Scrappy Improv
QUILTING

22 Mini Quilts to Make with Easy Piecing

T0322906

KELLY YOUNG

Landauer Publishing

Scrappy Improv Quilting

Landauer Publishing, www.landauerpub.com, is an imprint of Fox Chapel Publishing Company, Inc.

Copyright © 2021 by Kelly Young and Fox Chapel Publishing Company, Inc., 903 Square Street, Mount Joy, PA 17552.

Project Team
Editorial Director: Kerry Bogert
Editor: Amy Deputato
Copy Editor: Jean Bissell
Designer: Wendy Reynolds

ISBN 978-1-947163-62-1

Library of Congress Control Number: 2021935571

We are always looking for talented authors. To submit an idea, please send a brief inquiry to acquisitions@foxchapelpublishing.com.

Printed in China
24 23 22 21   2 4 6 8 10 9 7 5 3 1

This book has been published with the intent to provide accurate and authoritative information in regard to the subject matter within. While every precaution has been taken in the preparation of this book, the author and publisher expressly disclaim any responsibility for any errors, omissions, or adverse effects arising from the use or application of the information contained herein.

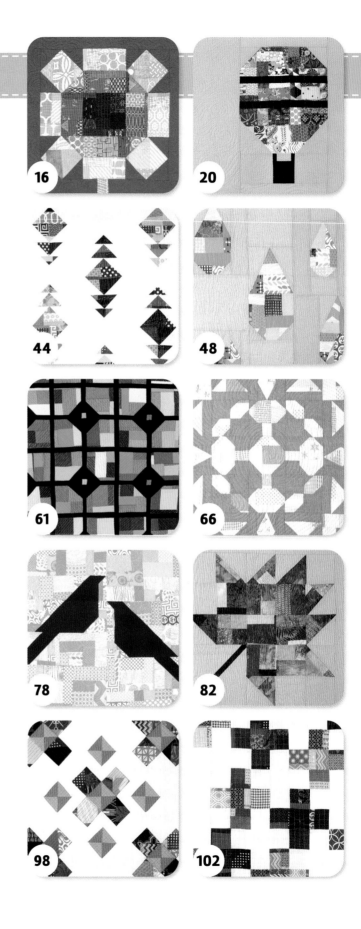

16
20
44
48
61
66
78
82
98
102

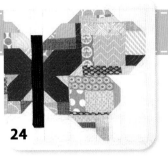

24

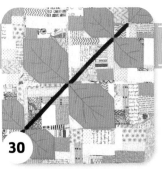

30

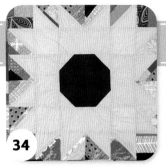

34

38

52

56

Contents

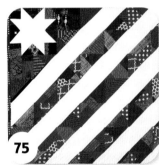

75

70

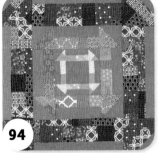

86

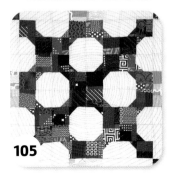

105

94

108

Scrap Savvy

Scraps, scraps, and more scraps! I don't know very many quilters who aren't bursting at the seams with them, and sometimes it's hard to figure out what to do with all of them. That's where *structured improvisation* comes in—this technique allows you to play with your scraps using improvisational, or unplanned, piecing. I'll show you how to do it, and it's quicker and easier than you think! Then, you'll use your new improv "fabric" with other solids or prints, following a step-by-step, traditional quilt pattern. The result is a one-of-a-kind scrap masterpiece that is uniquely yours.

All of the designs in this book are mini quilts, which makes them perfect for dipping your toes into improv piecing if you're apprehensive, and they're great projects for beginning quilters as well. No small project can be that scary, right?

I'll admit it—there was a time in my quilting life when I didn't understand the point of mini quilts. Even though I found them fun and satisfying to make because they are small and quick, I struggled with how to use them once they were finished. I've since come to appreciate all the ways in which mini quilts are awesome.

Color and print variations are practically endless, and that's the beauty of this method. Your own scraps will result in a quilt that is unique to you. You might choose a different background fabric for a specific project, or even a different colorway altogether. I've included color notes at the beginning of each project to help you choose scraps, but ultimately you will make these projects your own!

So . . . what can you do with mini quilts?

- Think of them as art—because they are! Anywhere you would hang a painting or picture, you can hang a mini quilt. Chapter 6 includes instructions for a hanging sleeve (see page 118) to make it easy to display your mini quilts. From nurseries, dens, and bedrooms to classrooms and office reception areas, any open wall space is a great spot for a mini quilt.
- Use them in a tablescape. Smaller mini quilts look great as placemats, and larger ones are perfect as table toppers, creating a beautiful foundation for any table setting.
- Drape them over an entry table or the backs of chairs. Mini quilts are a great way to make a room more inviting and welcoming.
- Turn them into throw pillows for a sofa or bed. The Finishing Your Quilt section includes detailed instructions for turning your finished mini quilts into pillows (see page 118) to make your space look extra cozy.
- Use them to give your home a pop of seasonal décor. Several of the quilts in this book are seasonal, and mini quilts give your home a little touch of the holidays without too much fuss.
- Give them as gifts. Handmade mini quilts are heartfelt treasures for friends, new babies, teachers, or anyone who needs a little extra happy!

CHAPTER 1

Tools, Tips, and Techniques

The structured improvisation technique uses fabric scraps, so this book assumes that readers have basic sewing knowledge, but don't worry if you are new to quilting or just new to improv piecing. I will cover everything you need to know to make the included projects from start to finish. Get ready to have some fun!

Tools of the Trade

Sewing machine: It's helpful to have a ¼" (0.5cm) foot, a walking foot, and a free-motion or darning foot.

Rotary cutter: Improv piecing creates a lot of seams that you'll need to slice through easily, so be sure to have a fresh, sharp blade.

Acrylic ruler: Have a 24" (61cm) ruler on hand for rotary cutting.

Cutting mat: Get the biggest mat your space will allow. You can thank me later!

Cotton thread: Use high-quality thread; my favorite is Aurifil 50 wt.

Straight pins and pincushion: Straight pins are helpful for holding pieces in place while sewing them together.

Scissors: The scissors you use for trimming improv pieces as you work don't need to be fancy, they just need to be sharp!

Seam ripper: A seam ripper is a necessary tool for fixing mistakes.

Iron and ironing board: Use your iron's hottest setting when pressing your finished improv pieces and mini quilts.

Starch or starch alternative: I prefer using starch or a starch alternative over steam to keep my improv pieces crisp and easy to work with.

Safety pins: Use safety pins for basting; larger ones are easier to manipulate.

Painter's or masking tape: Use tape for basting and for the tape-guided method (see page 9) of corner-to-corner sewing.

Marking pencil: Use a pencil for the line-guided method (see page 9) of corner-to-corner sewing.

Scrappy Piecing Perfection

When working with smaller pieces, it's very helpful to keep everything nice and neat, which makes it much easier to put your mini quilt together. Here are a few tips:

- **Prepare your fabric.** Press your fabric with a dry iron and either starch or starch alternative. The fabric will keep its shape, which makes it easier to handle and make precise cuts.
- **Cut your pieces accurately.** On a small piece, even a very slight miscut can make a difference.
- **Shorten your stitch length.** Shorter stitches will give you more control when lining up pieces.
- **When in doubt, use pins.** If you find that certain pieces are a little trickier to line up, pin them in place before sewing.

Seam Allowance

A ¼" (0.5cm) seam allowance is standard for quilting, and the patterns in this book are aligned with this standard. The instructions for each quilt require the pieces to be joined with a ¼" (0.5cm) seam allowance, with fabric right sides together.

An accurate ¼" (0.5cm) seam is especially important with smaller piecing. If you're having trouble keeping your seams consistent, try using a ¼" (0.5cm) piecing foot or switching to a thinner thread. Practice on some scraps, and you'll soon find that sewing accurate ¼" (0.5cm) seams becomes second nature.

Pressing Matters

When working with smaller pieces, a tiny inconsistency can cause a big problem. To avoid this, I always press throughout the piecing process with a dry iron, using starch or starch alternative. I'm careful not to rub my iron back and forth over my fabric, which could cause distortion. Sometimes you can inadvertently press a little fold into a seam, which can cause the piece to be too small. Give the block a finger press to make sure it is completely opened before using the iron to help get rid of those little folds.

You'll notice that pressing instructions are not included with these projects, and that is not an oversight. The randomness of improvisation means that improv blocks are turned in every direction, making it virtually impossible to nest seams. So, what can you do?

- **Press seams open.** If you want your quilt to lay perfectly flat, pressing each and every seam open is the only option. It takes a lot of time and effort, though, and there is a better way!
- **Keep seams consistently pressed to the side.** While you're piecing, pay attention to the direction in which the seam lies. When you join pieces together, make sure the seams stay flat. Use your finger to flip them if necessary while you sew, as this ensures the seams aren't twisted. With this method, the seams will be *almost* as flat as if you had pressed them open, and you won't have to press after every seam!
- **In general, press away from the bulk.** When joining improv with a solid fabric, press the seam toward the solid to help the block lie flat, and *always* listen to your pieces. Let the seam tell you which way it naturally wants to go.

Corner-to-Corner Sewing

Corner-to-corner sewing is required to create many of the projects in this book. These corners, also known as snowball corners or stitch-and-flip corners, are a basic building block of quilting, and they can be used to create amazing shapes or a curvy illusion within a quilt. There are a couple of different methods for sewing these corners, so choose the method you're more comfortable with.

Line-guided method: This is the traditional way to sew snowball corners. With this method, use a marking pencil to draw a diagonal line on the wrong side of the corner square as shown. Then sew corner to corner, using the drawn line as a guide.

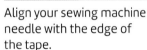

Wrong side of fabric

Line-Guided Method

Align your sewing machine needle with the edge of the tape.

Keep the corners aligned on the edge of the tape while sewing.

Tape-Guided Method

Tape-guided method: This is my favorite method for sewing these corners. It is much faster because there is no drawing involved, but it is just as accurate as the more traditional method.

First, align a piece of painter's tape or masking tape with the needle of your sewing machine as shown. Be sure the tape doesn't cover your feed dogs. Then place the top corner of the square under your presser foot, with the corner aligned with your needle. Align the bottom corner with the edge of the painter's tape and begin sewing. Take your time and keep the bottom corner aligned with the tape while you sew. Sew all the way across the square and then marvel at your perfectly straight line!

At first, it might feel odd to sew without the drawn line to guide you, but don't give up on this method. It won't take long before you feel comfortable with it, and then you'll be able to sew those corners in a flash.

Whatever method you choose, once you have the corners sewn according to the pattern instructions, you will need to trim them. Using scissors or a rotary cutter, trim each corner ¼" (0.5cm) from the seam (for seam allowance) and then press the corner open. The block is then ready to be used in the mini quilt.

Different Block Methods

We quilters are creatures of habit, and many of us have our favorite ways of making basic quilting units like flying geese or half-square triangles (HSTs)—including me! So, while the project instructions include *my* favorite methods of making the required blocks, if you prefer another way to make a particular unit, just adjust the pattern measurements accordingly.

Triangle-in-a-Square Blocks

Several of the mini quilts in this book require a triangle-in-a-square ruler set, which is different from a 60-degree pyramid ruler. The triangle in this ruler is narrower at the bottom, and the set comes with both a main triangle ruler and a side unit ruler, which enables the triangle to be pieced into a square block. These rulers are widely available from several different brands, are easy to use, and are great for helping you easily cut and piece triangle-in-a-square blocks with no fabric waste.

Follow these steps to piece perfect triangle-in-a-square units:

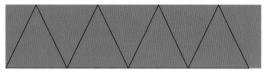

1. Cut a strip of fabric the width specified in the pattern instructions. Leave the fabric folded from selvage to selvage.
2. Align the blunt tip of the ruler with the top of the strip, then cut the triangle. Because the fabric is folded, one cut will yield two triangles.
3. After cutting, rotate the ruler to align it with the cut edge to cut the next triangles. Continue moving the ruler and cutting until all needed pieces are cut.
4. Cut the triangle side units using the same method. When cutting side units, be sure to leave the fabric folded so that each cut yields two *mirror-image units.*

Note: Fat quarters and improv pieces can be cut using the same procedure. Just be sure to cut your strips to the correct width and let the rulers do the rest!

A triangle-in-a-square ruler set simplifies the process of making these blocks.

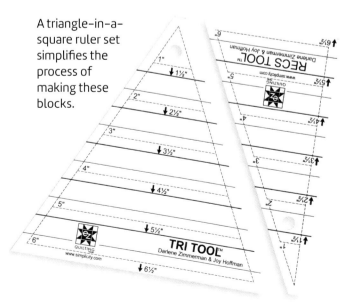

Improv Piecing Made Easy

Before jumping right into making your favorite mini quilts in this book, you first need to learn how to piece your scraps together using improvisation. The improv units add texture, interest, and a one-of-a-kind look to each quilt that just can't be achieved using single fabrics.

Improv piecing is meant to be relaxing and fun, without too many rules to stifle the process. So put away your seam rippers, pins, rotary cutters, and rulers while sewing your scraps together. You'll definitely need these tools for sewing your quilt once your improv piece is finished, but when working through your scraps, just use your scissors to cut and let go of the rest.

Press and Sort Your Scraps

Most of these mini quilts require only a handful or two of scraps, but don't skip the important steps of preparing and organizing them before you begin a project. Give the scraps a quick press before sewing so they are easier to handle, then sort your scraps by size. Because these are small quilts, use the smaller scraps to keep everything in proportion. You don't need to measure; just use your hand as a guide and make three piles. I name my scrap piles to keep myself organized:

- **Bits:** Square or rectangular scraps smaller than the palm of your hand (not including your fingers)
- **Pieces:** Scraps that are larger than bits, up to the length of your whole hand
- **Strings:** Skinny scraps that are longer than your hand, up to about 12" (30.5cm) long

If you lack smaller scraps, or if your scrap strips are very long, just use your scissors to cut a piece or two off your larger scraps until you have a good pile of each size.

Sorting first saves a lot of time while sewing. By taking time to sort, you won't find yourself searching for a piece that is the right size while joining your scraps together.

Sparkle and Depth

When choosing scraps for your mini quilt, don't ignore the lightest and darkest fabrics. Mixing a wide variety of prints and shades gives the improv piece texture and variation. The lightest scraps give the illusion of light sparkling through the piece, while the deepest tones add depth, and you want your piece to have both.

Building the Improv Units

Start by sewing together two different scrap bits from your pile. Repeat this process three times to yield four total units with as much fabric variety as possible. Then add another scrap to each unit. Trim off any excess length from all four units. Finally, add a fourth scrap to each improv unit and again trim off any excess length. As you add pieces to each improv unit, choose from whichever scrap pile is closest to the size you need.

Note: When adding scraps to a unit, don't worry about making the pieces fit perfectly. If they're a little too long, that's OK—just put the trimmings back into your scrap piles. You don't have to throw a scrap away until you decide it's too small.

Once you have four improv units with four scraps in each unit, join them together. If you need to add a piece to make one unit fit with another, that's OK. Then you'll be ready to join more bits and start the whole process again. Keep working through your scrap piles and joining improv units in this way until you have an improv piece that measures the required size specified in the quilt pattern.

1. Sew sets of two bits together.

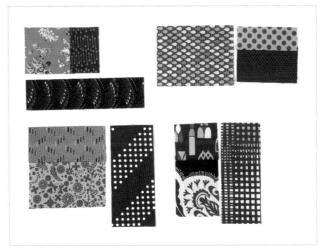

2. Trim the excess length and lay out a third scrap piece.

Cutting and Organizing

Don't get discouraged by the cutting list for some of these patterns—the process is not as daunting as it might look! Some of the patterns require several different-sized pieces, but because they are mini quilts, there might be only one or two pieces needed of a certain size. You'll be cutting pieces of several sizes from each strip of fabric to minimize the amount of fabric required for each project, and the cutting list is ordered to make the most of each strip. Just take your time when cutting, and keep your pieces organized with sticky notes, baggies, or even paper plates for each size, and you'll be ready to go!

3. Sew the third scrap piece to each unit.

4. Trim the excess, then choose a fourth scrap for each unit.

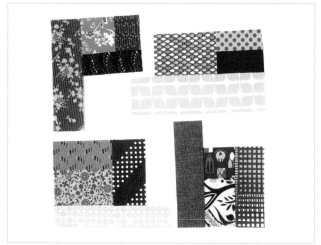

5. Sew the fourth scrap piece to each unit and trim to fit.

6. Join the units to make two larger units. Add another scrap if you need to make them fit together.

7. Join the two larger pieces together, adding a scrap to fit if needed.

8. The finished improv piece.

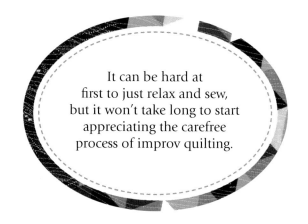

It can be hard at first to just relax and sew, but it won't take long to start appreciating the carefree process of improv quilting.

Keep It Irregular

Adding scraps all in one direction will make a block that looks like a rail fence block, and adding scraps evenly around the center will make the block look more like a log cabin. Instead, add scraps to each unit as randomly as possible, varying the horizontal and vertical seams. When joining your improv units, rotate the pieces to make the seams disjointed, which also adds to the random look.

Rectangles, Squares, and Strips

By far, most of my scraps tend to be rectangles, squares, and strips, which means that my improv pieces contain primarily right angles. Anytime I have oddly shaped scraps, I prefer to trim them to make them easier to work with. However, you certainly can use triangles or other irregularly shaped scraps if you want. Just piece the shapes together and then square up your improv unit accordingly.

Scrap Shortage?

I know it's unlikely that any of these mini quilts will wipe out your scrap bins, but sometimes you'll have a shortage of certain colors. If your heart is set on making a certain quilt with a color that you don't have, you can supplement your scraps a few different ways. My favorite way is to have a scrap swap with a quilty friend. If that's not possible, either cut pieces from a few fabrics in your stash, or purchase a few new fabrics. Most quilt shops will not cut anything smaller than ¼ yard (22.9cm), so I usually purchase ⅓ yard (30.5cm) and cut a strip to use as "scraps," leaving a full ¼ yard (22.9cm) for another project.

Slice and Shuffle

Remember that the pieces for the blocks in your mini quilt will come from your improv piece, and the scraps will likely be cut during this process, but if you decide that your finished improv piece is a little too chunky, and you would rather have smaller scrap pieces, there's an easy fix. Just use your rotary cutter to slice the entire piece into regular squares, shuffle them, and sew them back together. The whole piece will end up a little smaller because of the seams, but this is a fast way to break up larger scraps within your improv piece.

Ignore the Rules

Ultimately, these are all just guidelines to help you on your way. There really is no right or wrong way to sew your scraps together. If you find a method that feels comfortable for you, go with it. As long as you end up with an improv piece that is the appropriate size for your quilt, you can't go wrong. And don't forget to relax and have fun with it!

CHAPTER 2

Single-Block Beauties

If you're new to the improv game, single-block quilts are a great way to start playing with the process. Whether the improv pieces are color-controlled designs or multi-colored explosions, whether they're in the background or featured in the block units, a single focal point is a great way to make a big impact with just a little effort.

Summer Blossom

Rolling Stone quilt blocks are a great way to add a curvy illusion to a quilt without actually having to tackle curved piecing. In the Summer Blossom quilt, the rounded shape is perfect for a single bold bloom. This cheerful quilt is sure to brighten any spot where it hangs.

Color notes: Summer Blossom plays with warm, tropical colors to create a quilt that draws you right in. I used the warmest berry purple—almost pink—scraps in the center of the block for the tropical feel, and the oranges and yellows keep the quilt bright and sunny. The darker blue background may seem like an unlikely choice, but the deeper color makes the flower appear much more vivid.

MATERIALS

With the exception of improv pieces, yardage is based on 42" (106.7cm)–wide fabric.

- One improv piece, 5" x 5" (12.7 x 12.7cm), pieced from assorted berry purple scraps for block
- One improv piece, 4" x 9" (10.2 x 22.9cm), pieced from assorted green scraps for block
- One improv piece, 8" x 10" (20.3 x 25.4cm), pieced from assorted orange scraps for block
- One improv piece, 9" x 14" (22.9 x 35.6cm), pieced from assorted yellow scraps for block
- ⅓ yard (30.5cm) medium blue fabric for blocks and background (Robert Kaufman Fabrics' Kona® Cotton in Delft is shown)
- ¼ yard (22.9cm) berry-colored fabric for binding
- ⅔ yard (61cm) fabric for backing, or backing measuring 20" x 28" (50.8 x 71.1cm)
- 20" x 28" (50.8 x 71.1cm) piece of batting

CUTTING

All measurements include ¼" (0.5cm) seam allowances.

From the berry purple improv piece, cut:
- One square, 4½" (11.4cm)

From the green improv piece, cut:
- One square, 3½" (8.9cm)
- Three rectangles, 1½" x 4" (3.8 x 10.2cm)

From the orange improv piece, cut:
- Four rectangles, 2½" x 4½" (6.4 x 11.4cm)
- Four squares, 2½" (6.4cm)

From the yellow improv piece, cut:
- Four rectangles, 2½" x 4½" (6.4 x 11.4cm)
- Four squares, 4½" (11.4cm)

From the blue background fabric, cut:
- One strip, 2½" x 42" (6.4 x 106.7cm); subcut:
  - Two rectangles, 2½" x 12½" (6.4 x 31.8cm)
  - One rectangle, 2½" x 16½" (6.4 x 41.9cm)
- One strip, 8" x 42" (20.3 x 106.7cm); subcut:
  - One rectangle, 8" x 10½" (20.3 x 26.7cm)
  - One rectangle, 8" x 4½" (20.3 x 11.4cm)
  - One rectangle, 8" x 3½" (20.3 x 8.9cm)
  - One rectangle 3½" x 5½" (8.9 x 14cm)
  - Twelve squares, 2½" (6.4cm)
  - Two squares, 2" (5.1cm)

From the binding fabric, cut:
- Three strips, 2½" x 42" (6.4 x 106.7cm), for binding

FINISHED QUILT SIZE: 16" X 24" (40.6 X 61CM)

Note that improv pieces are represented by solid colors. Refer to page 9 for corner-to-corner sewing methods.

Make the Flower Block

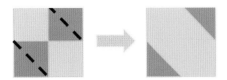

1. Place two 2½" (6.4cm) blue squares on opposite corners of one 4½" (11.4cm) yellow improv square, right sides together, and sew from corner to corner. Trim away the excess fabric, leaving ¼" (0.5cm) seam allowance, and press open.

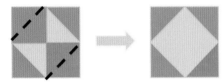

2. Repeat this process, sewing a 2½" (6.4cm) blue square and an orange improv square to the remaining corners of the square to complete one corner unit. Make four total corner units for the flower block.

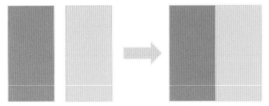

3. Sew one 2½" x 4½" (6.4 x 11.4cm) yellow improv rectangle and one 2½" x 4½" (6.4 x 11.4cm) orange improv rectangle to make one side unit. Make four total side units.

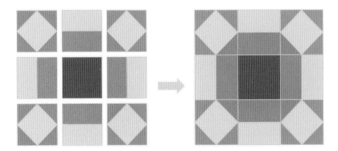

4. Lay out the four corner units, four side units, and 4½" (11.4cm) berry purple improv square into three rows as shown, using the 4½" (11.4cm) berry purple square in the center of the block, and sew the block together. The block should measure 12½" (31.8cm), including seam allowances.

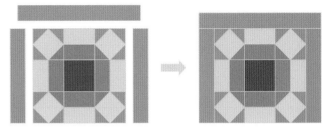

5. Sew one blue 2½" x 12½" (6.4 x 31.8cm) rectangle to each side of the block, then sew one 2½" x 16½" (6.4 x 41.9cm) rectangle to the top of the block.

Make the Stem Unit

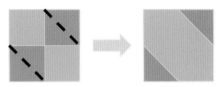

6. Place two 2" (5.1cm) blue squares on opposite corners of the 3½" (8.9cm) green improv square, right sides together, and sew from corner to corner. Trim away the excess fabric, leaving ¼" (0.5cm) seam allowance, and press open to create the leaf.

7. Sew the three 1½" x 4" (3.8 x 10.2cm) green improv rectangles end to end to create one long flower stem. Trim the stem to 10½" (26.7cm) long.

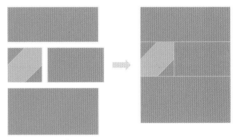

8. Lay out the leaf and the 3½" x 5½" (8.9 x 14cm) blue rectangle, 3½" x 8" (8.9 x 20.3cm) blue rectangle, and 4½" x 8" (11.4 x 20.3cm) blue rectangle, then join the pieces together.

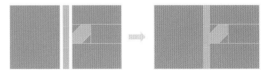

9. Sew the stem to the 8" x 10½" (20.3 x 26.7cm) blue rectangle, then sew the two halves of the stem unit.

Assemble the Quilt Top

10. Referring to the quilt assembly diagram, sew the flower block to the top of the stem unit.

Finish the Quilt

Refer to Finishing Your Quilt on page 112 for instructions on basting, quilting, and binding your quilt.

11. Cut the backing fabric into one length, measuring 20" x 28" (50.8 x 71.1cm) to make the backing.

12. Layer the backing, batting, and quilt top and baste the layers together. Hand- or machine-quilt as desired. Summer Blossom is quilted with a dense crosshatch design in the center of the flower, radiating lines in the orange and yellow petals, and swirls in the background.

13. Use the 2½" (6.4cm)–wide berry purple strips to make the binding, then attach it to the quilt.

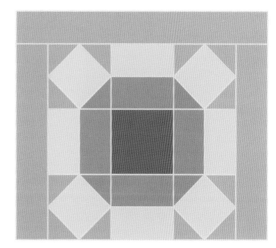

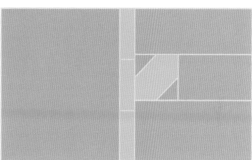

Quilt assembly diagram

The different quilting motifs in each color add great definition to the flower.

Backing fabric and binding on the finished quilt.

Up, Up, and Away

Unlike seeing airplanes or helicopters, spotting a hot air balloon in the sky is a rare treat. A balloon's quiet presence is mesmerizing, and it has always amazed me that something so majestic can be powered with the simple use of heat. In this quilt, the hot air balloon is offset, giving it the feeling of floating off into the distance.

Color notes: The improv in this hot air balloon covers a relatively small area, but it really packs a punch. Because the improv is concentrated in one spot, it is a great place to showcase a handful of your most special scraps. The blue background fabric is the vibrant sky blue of a cloudless day, and it really shows off the scraps used in the balloon.

MATERIALS

With the exception of improv pieces, yardage is based on 42" (106.7cm)–wide fabric.

- One improv piece, 13" x 15" (33 x 38.1cm), pieced from assorted multi-colored scraps for block
- ½ yard (45.7cm) blue fabric for block and background (Robert Kaufman Fabrics' Kona® Cotton in Prairie Sky is shown)
- ⅛ yard (11.4cm) black fabric for block
- ¼ yard (22.9cm) fabric for binding, or refer to page 117 to create a scrappy pieced binding measuring 104" (2.6m)
- ¾ yard (68.6cm) fabric for backing, or backing measuring 27" x 27" (68.6 x 68.6cm)
- 27" x 27" (68.6 x 68.6cm) piece of batting

CUTTING

All measurements include ¼" (0.5cm) seam allowances.

From the improv piece, cut:
- One rectangle, 13" x 15" (33 x 38.1cm)

From the black fabric, cut:
- One square, 3½" (8.9cm)
- Two rectangles, 1½" x 13½" (3.8 x 34.3cm)
- Two rectangles, 1" x 1½" (2.5 x 3.8cm)

From the blue background fabric, cut:
- One strip, 5" x 42" (12.7 x 106.7cm); subcut:
  - Two squares, 5" (12.7cm)
  - Two rectangles, 4½" x 5" (11.4 x 12.7cm)
  - Two squares, 3½" (8.9cm)
  - One rectangle, 1½" x 2½" (3.8 x 6.4cm)
- One strip, 9½" x 42" (24.1 x 106.7cm); subcut:
  - One rectangle, 9½" x 24½" (24.1 x 62.2cm)
  - One rectangle, 4½" x 12½" (11.4 x 31.8cm)
  - One rectangle, 2½" x 12½" (6.4 x 31.8cm)
- One strip, 3½" x 42" (8.9 x 106.7cm); subcut:
  - One rectangle, 3½" x 24½" (8.9 x 62.2cm)

For a solid binding, from the binding fabric, cut:
- Three strips, 2½" x 42" (6.4 x 106.7cm), for binding

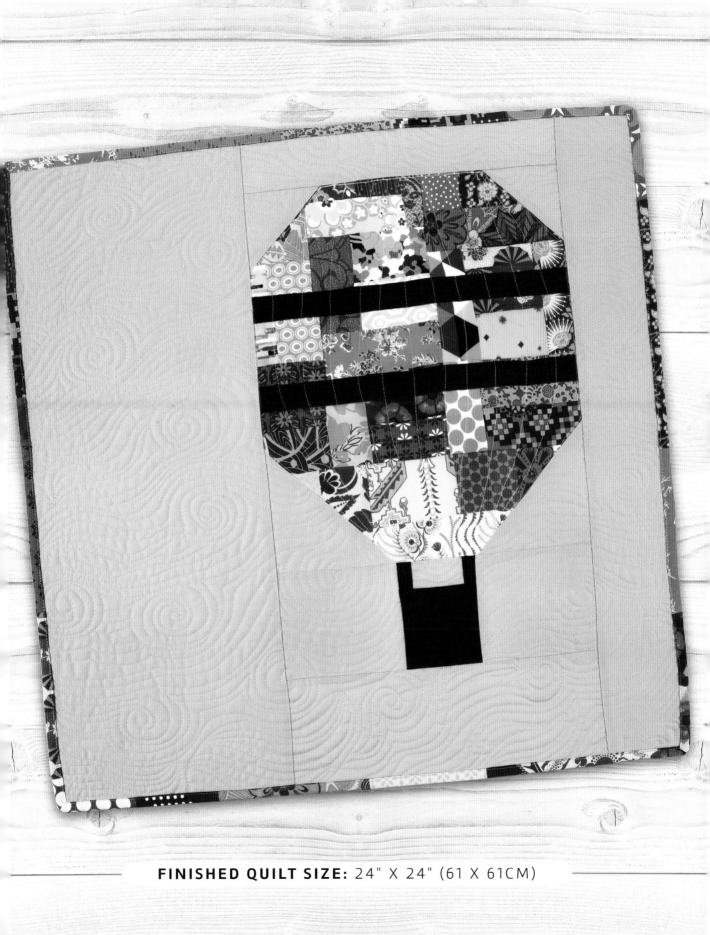

FINISHED QUILT SIZE: 24" X 24" (61 X 61CM)

Note that improv pieces are represented by solid colors. Refer to page 9 for corner-to-corner sewing methods.

Make the Hot Air Balloon Block

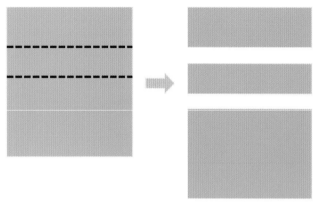

1. Cut the improv piece horizontally across the short side. Make one cut approximately 5" (12.7cm) from the top and make a second cut approximately 7½" (19.1cm) from the top.

The exact location of the two cuts is not important—they just need to be straight and placed toward the upper center of the improv piece.

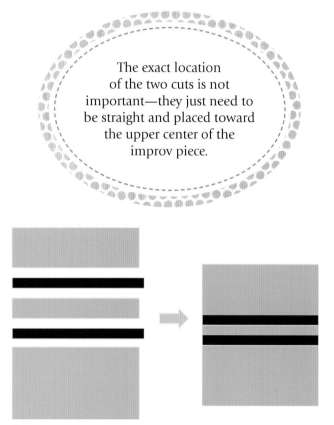

2. Sew one 1½" x 13½" (3.8 x 34.3cm) black rectangle between each of the cut pieces to create the stripes on the balloon. Keeping the stripes straight, trim the finished piece to 12½" x 14½" (31.8 x 36.8cm).

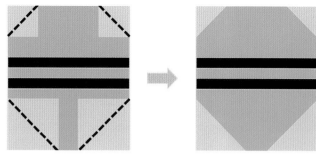

3. Place two 3½" (8.9cm) blue squares on the top corners of the improv rectangle and sew from corner to corner. Using the same process, sew the two 5" (12.7cm) blue squares to the bottom two corners of the improv piece. Trim away the excess fabric from all four corners, leaving ¼" (0.5cm) seam allowance, and press open to complete the top of the hot air balloon block.

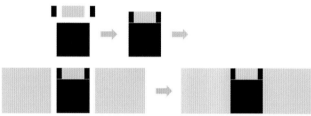

4. Lay out two 1 x 1½" (2.5 x 3.8cm) black rectangles, one 1½" x 2½" (3.8 x 6.4cm) blue rectangle, and one 3½" (8.9cm) black square as shown. Join the pieces together to complete the hanging basket, then sew one 4½" x 5" (11.4 x 12.7cm) blue rectangle to each side of the hanging basket.

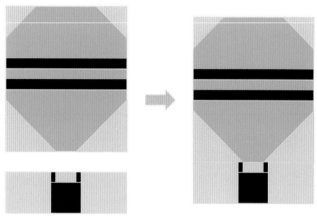

5. Sew the top of the hot air balloon to the hanging basket to complete the quilt block.

Assemble the Quilt Top

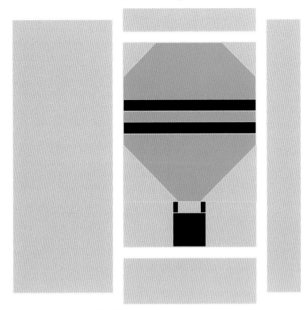

Quilt assembly diagram

6. Referring to the quilt assembly diagram, sew the 2½" x 12½" (6.4 x 31.8cm) blue rectangle to the top of the block, then sew the 4½" x 12½" (11.4 x 31.8cm) blue rectangle to the bottom of the block. Next, sew the 3½" x 24½" (8.9 x 62.2cm) blue rectangle to the right side of the block, then sew the 9½" x 24½" (24.1 x 62.2cm) blue rectangle to the left side of the block to complete the quilt top.

Finish the Quilt

Refer to Finishing Your Quilt on page 112 for instructions on basting, quilting, and binding your quilt.

7. Cut the backing fabric into one piece, measuring 27" x 27" (68.6 x 68.6cm).

8. Layer the backing, batting, and quilt top and baste the layers together. Hand- or machine-quilt as desired. The balloon in Up, Up, and Away is quilted with vertical curved lines to give the block a rounded, puffy look. The hanging basket is quilted with a dense crosshatch design, and the background is quilted with a blowing wind motif, which gives the quilt plenty of movement.

9. Use the 2½" (6.4cm)–wide binding fabric or scrap strips to make the binding, then attach it to the quilt.

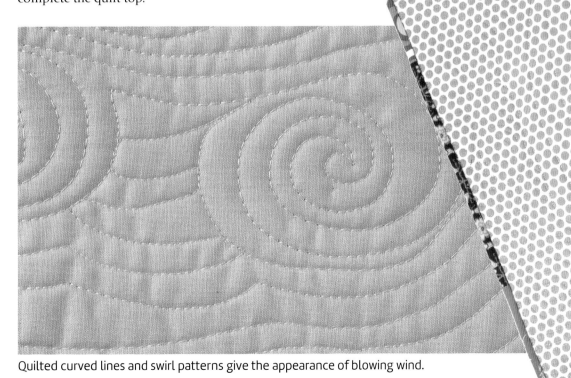

Backing fabric and binding on the finished quilt.

Quilted curved lines and swirl patterns give the appearance of blowing wind.

Flutter

Butterflies have a variety of shapes and almost endless colors. The patterns in their delicate wings are so lovely, and piecing the wings with scraps is a great way to recreate their color variation and texture. This butterfly has its wings open wide, giving it a unique shape.

Color notes: Yellow and orange are neighbors on the color wheel, and that makes them very easy to pair in this quilt. Purple and pink, or blue and teal, are other great options. Or pick a favorite color and use two different shades to create a gradient effect.

MATERIALS

With the exception of improv pieces, yardage is based on 42" (106.7cm)–wide fabric.

- One improv piece, 10" x 18" (25.4 x 45.7cm), pieced from assorted yellow and orange scraps for block
- ⅛ yard (11.4cm) orange fabric for block (Robert Kaufman Fabrics' Kona® Cotton in Tangerine is shown)
- ⅓ yard (30.5 cm) cream fabric for block and background (Robert Kaufman Fabrics' Kona® Cotton in Bone is shown)
- ¼ yard (22.9cm) dark gray fabric for block and binding (Robert Kaufman Fabrics' Kona® Cotton in Charcoal is shown)
- ½ yard (45.7cm) fabric for backing, or backing measuring 18" x 24" (45.7 x 61cm)
- 18" x 24" (45.7 x 61cm) piece of batting

CUTTING

All measurements include ¼" (0.5cm) seam allowances.

From the yellow and orange improv piece, cut:
- Two rectangles, 4½" x 5½" (11.4 x 14cm)
- Two rectangles, 3½" x 4½" (8.9 x 11.4cm)
- Six rectangles, 1½" x 2½" (3.8 x 6.4cm)
- Two rectangles, 2½" x 3½" (6.4 x 8.9cm)
- Two rectangles, 1½" x 4½" (3.8 x 11.4cm)
- Eight squares, 1½" (3.8cm)

From the orange fabric, cut:
- Two rectangles, 2½" x 3½" (6.4 x 8.9cm)
- Two squares, 2½" (6.4cm)

From the dark gray fabric, cut:
- One rectangle, 1½" x 7½" (3.8 x 19.1cm)
- Two strips, 2½" x 42" (6.4 x 106.7cm), for binding

From the cream fabric, cut:
- One strip, 5½" x 42" (14 x 106.7cm); subcut:
  - Two rectangles, 2½" x 5½" (6.4 x 14cm)
  - Two squares, 2½" (6.4cm)
  - Nine rectangles, 1½" x 2½" (3.8 x 6.4cm)
  - Four squares, 2" (5.1cm)
  - Fifteen squares, 1½" (3.8cm)
  - Two squares, 1" (2.5cm)
- One strip, 2" x 42" (2.5 x 106.7cm); subcut:
  - Two rectangles, 2" x 10½" (2.5 x 26.7cm), for side borders
- One strip, 2½" x 42" (6.4 x 106.7cm); subcut:
  - Two rectangles, 2½" x 20½" (6.4 x 52.1cm), for top and bottom borders

FINISHED QUILT SIZE: 14" X 20" (35.6 X 50.8CM)

Note that improv pieces are represented by solid colors. Refer to page 9 for corner-to-corner sewing methods.

Make the Block

Note: This quilt requires sewing a mirror image of each component to create the two halves of the butterfly. Each step will include directions for sewing one part of the wing, and then its mirror image, in the same step.

1. Place two 1½" (3.8cm) cream squares on the corners of one 1½" x 4½" (3.8 x 11.4cm) improv rectangle and sew from corner to corner. Trim the excess fabric, leaving ¼" (0.5cm) seam allowance, and press open. Make two total units.

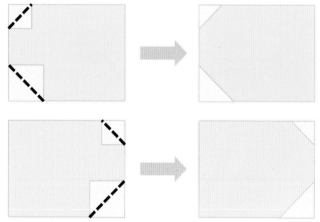

2. Place a 1½" (3.8cm) cream square on the top left corner of one 4½" x 5½" (11.4 x 14cm) improv rectangle. Then place a 2" (5.1cm) cream square on the bottom left corner and sew from corner to corner. Trim the excess fabric, leaving ¼" (0.5cm) seam allowance, and press open. Sew a 1½" (3.8cm) cream square to the top right corner of the remaining 4½" x 5½" (11.4 x 14cm) rectangle, then sew a 2" (5.1cm) cream square to the bottom right corner of the rectangle to create a mirror-image unit.

3. Place a 2" (5.1cm) cream square on the top right corner of one 2½" x 3½" (6.4 x 8.9cm) improv rectangle and sew from corner to corner. Trim the excess fabric, leaving ¼" (0.5cm) seam allowance, and press open. Then sew a 2" (5.1cm) cream square to the top left corner of the remaining 2½" x 3½" (6.4 x 8.9cm) improv rectangle to make a mirror-image unit.

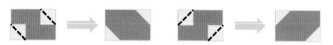

4. Place two 1½" (3.8cm) improv squares on opposite corners of one 2½" x 3½" (6.4 x 8.9cm) orange rectangle and sew from corner to corner. Trim the excess fabric, leaving ¼" (0.5cm) seam allowance, and press open. Repeat this process, using the second 2½" x 3½" (6.4 x 8.9cm) orange rectangle, and sew two remaining 1½" (3.8cm) improv squares to the opposite two corners to make a mirror-image unit.

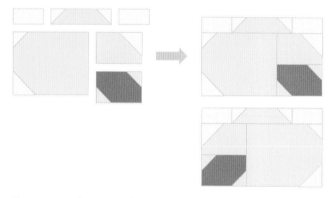

5. Lay out the units from steps 1–4 plus two 1½" x 2½" (3.8 x 6.4cm) cream rectangles, then join the pieces together to create the wing top. Use the mirror-image units created in steps 1–4 to create the second mirror-image wing top.

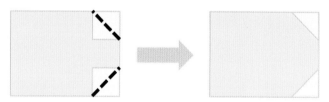

6. Place two 1½" (3.8cm) cream squares on the corners of one 3½" x 4½" (8.9 x 11.4cm) improv rectangle and sew from corner to corner. Trim the excess fabric, leaving ¼" (0.5cm) seam allowance, and press open. Make two identical units.

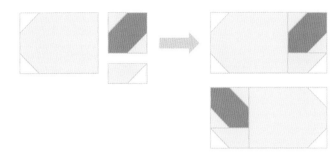

7. Place two 1½" (3.8cm) improv squares on opposite corners of one 2½" (6.4cm) orange square and sew from corner to corner. Trim the excess fabric, leaving ¼" (0.5cm) seam allowance, and press open. Make two identical units.

9. Lay out the units created in steps 6 and 7 and one 1½" x 2½" (3.8 x 6.4cm) unit from step 8 as shown. Join the pieces together to create one wing bottom. Use the mirror-image units to create a mirror-image wing bottom.

8. Place a 1½" (3.8cm) cream square on the corner of one 1½" x 2½" (3.8 x 6.4cm) improv rectangle and sew from corner to corner. Trim the excess fabric, leaving ¼" (0.5cm) seam allowance, and press open. Then sew a 1½" (3.8cm) cream square to the opposite corner of a 1½" x 2½" (3.8 x 6.4cm) improv rectangle to make a mirror-image unit. Make two of each mirror-image unit.

Pay close attention to the direction of the sewn corners for this quilt. Most of these pieces are rectangles, so they can't be rotated. If you're unsure, just open up the sewn corner to be sure it is sewn correctly before trimming.

10. Place a 1" (2.5cm) cream square on the corner of a 1½" x 2½" (3.8 x 6.4cm) improv rectangle and sew from corner to corner. Trim the excess fabric, leaving ¼" (0.5cm) seam allowance, and press open to make a wing tip. Then sew a 1" (2.5cm) cream square to the opposite corner of a 1½" x 2½" (3.8 x 6.4cm) improv rectangle to make a mirror-image wing tip.

11. Lay out the wing tip unit, one of the 1½" x 2½" (3.8 x 6.4cm) units created in step 8, two 1½" x 2½" (3.8 x 6.4cm) cream rectangles, and one 2½" (6.4cm) cream square as shown. Join the pieces together to make the wing tip, then use the mirror-image units to make the mirror-image wing tip.

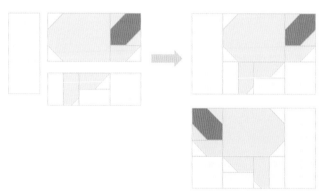

12. Sew the wing bottom and wing tip together. Then sew one 2½" x 5½" (6.4 x 14cm) cream rectangle to the outside of the wing to finish the bottom of the wing. Repeat this process to make a mirror-image unit.

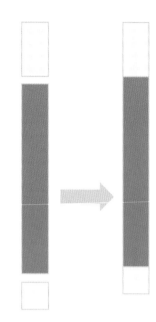

13. Sew a 1½" x 2½" (3.8 x 6.4cm) cream rectangle to the top of the 1½" x 7½" (3.8 x 19.1cm) dark gray rectangle. Then sew one 1½" (3.8cm) cream square to the bottom of the rectangle to create the butterfly body.

Graceful lines that follow the wing shape add softness to the butterfly's wings.

Assemble the Quilt Top

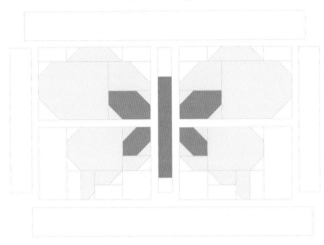

Quilt assembly diagram

14. Referring to the quilt assembly diagram, arrange the wing pieces and sew the top of the wing to the bottom of the wing. Repeat this process for the mirror-image wing top and bottom. Then sew the butterfly body between the two halves to complete the butterfly block.

15. Sew a 2" x 10½" (5.1 x 26.7cm) cream rectangle to each side of the butterfly block. Then sew a 2½" x 20½" (6.4 x 52.1cm) cream rectangle to the top and bottom of the butterfly block to complete the quilt top.

Finish the Quilt

Refer to Finishing Your Quilt on page 112 for instructions on basting, quilting, and binding your quilt.

16. Cut the backing fabric into one piece, measuring 18" x 24" (45.7 x 61cm).

17. Layer the backing, batting, and quilt top and baste the layers together. Hand- or machine-quilt as desired. Flutter is quilted with lines that echo the shape of the butterfly wings and body, with swirls in the background.

18. Use the 2½" (6.4cm)–wide dark gray strips to make the binding, then attach it to the quilt.

Backing fabric and binding on the finished quilt.

The swirls in the background give an impression of movement against the more linear quilting of the wings and body.

Botanics

When Earth wakes up from a long winter, spring makes its debut with fresh greenery and soft neutrals. The little green shoots poking through the ground and sprouting from trees are a promise of what's to come, and they invite us outside to enjoy the warmer weather.

Color notes: This quilt is the perfect place to use your neutral scraps. Shades of cream, tan, white, and even a little metallic gold are packed into the background, and two shades of green give the plant dimension. If you prefer a cooler look, choose shades of gray for the background instead of warmer beige and tan.

MATERIALS

With the exception of improv pieces, yardage is based on 42" (106.7cm)–wide fabric.

- Two improv pieces, 13" x 26" (33 x 66cm), pieced from assorted cream, tan, and beige scraps for background and blocks
- ¼ yard (22.9cm) light green fabric for blocks (Robert Kaufman Fabrics' Kona® Cotton in Tarragon is shown)
- ⅛ yard (11.4cm) dark green fabric for blocks (Robert Kaufman Fabrics' Kona® Cotton in Basil is shown)
- ¼ yard (22.9cm) tan fabric for binding (Robert Kaufman Fabrics' Kona® Cotton in Khaki is shown)
- ¾ yard (68.6cm) fabric for backing, or backing measuring 27" x 27" (68.6 x 68.6cm)
- 27" x 27" (68.6 x 68.6cm) piece of batting

CUTTING

All measurements include ¼" (0.5cm) seam allowances.

From the tan improv pieces, cut:
- Three squares, 7½" (19.1cm)
- Six squares, 6½" (16.5cm)
- Six rectangles, 2½" x 4½" (6.4 x 11.4cm)
- Four rectangles, 2½" x 6½" (6.4 x 16.5cm)
- Four squares, 2½" (6.4cm)
- One square, 3½" (8.9cm)
- Ten squares, 1½" (3.8cm)

From the light green fabric, cut:
- Five squares, 4½" (11.4cm)
- Two squares, 6½" (16.5cm)

From the dark green fabric, cut:
- Three rectangles, 1" x 12" (2.5 x 30.5cm)
- One rectangle, 1" x 6" (2.5 x 15.2cm)

From the tan fabric, cut:
- Three strips, 2½" x 42" (6.4 x 106.7cm), for binding

Instead of cutting 1½" (3.8cm) squares from improv pieces, you can choose to cut solid 1½" (3.8cm) squares from ten different scraps. They finish at just 1" (2.5cm), and, when sewn, they will blend right into the improv.

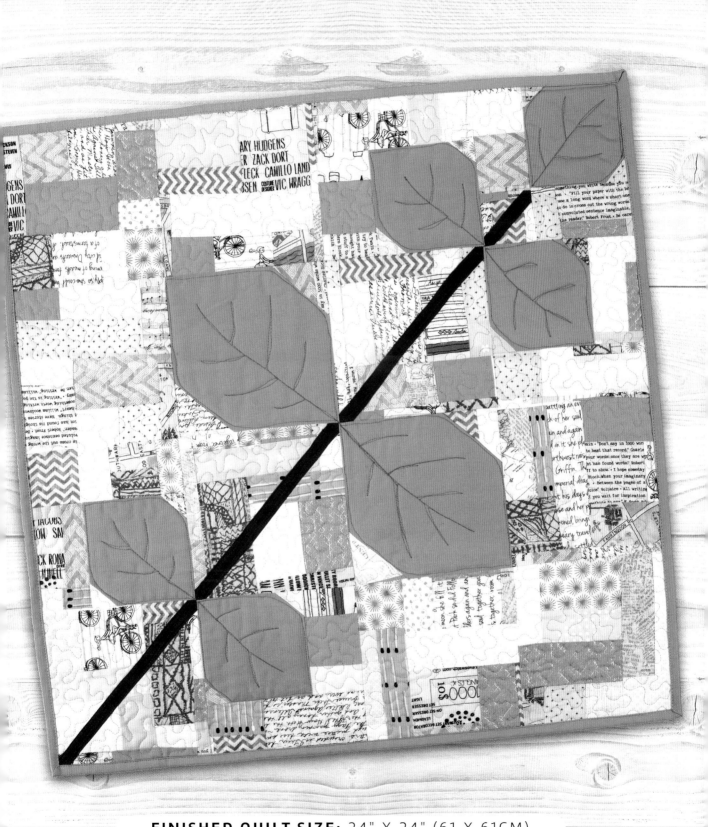

FINISHED QUILT SIZE: 24" X 24" (61 X 61CM)

Note that improv pieces are represented by solid colors. Refer to the corner-to-corner sewing methods on page 9.

Make the Stems

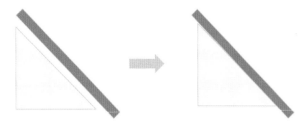

1. Cut a 7½" (19.1cm) tan improv square in half diagonally. Sew a 1" x 12" (2.5 x 30.5cm) dark green rectangle to one of the halves and press open.

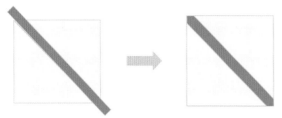

2. Sew the second half of the tan square to the other side of the dark green rectangle as shown. Press open and trim the stem unit to 6½" (16.5cm), keeping the dark green rectangle centered in the block. Make three 6½" (16.5cm) stem blocks.

3. Use the same process and cut the 3½" (8.9cm) tan improv square in half diagonally. Sew the 1" x 6" (2.5 x 15.2cm) dark green rectangle between the two halves to make one stem block trimmed to 2½" (6.4cm).

Fold the dark green rectangle and the cut piece of the tan improv square in half to find the center point of each piece. Use a pin to hold the dark green rectangle in place to keep it centered when sewing. Use a square ruler with a bias line to keep the dark green rectangle centered when trimming to size.

Make the Leaves

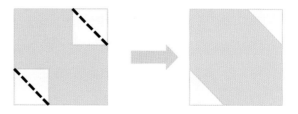

4. Place two 1½" (3.8cm) tan improv squares on opposite corners of one 4½" (11.4cm) light green square and sew from corner to corner. Trim the excess fabric, leaving ¼" (0.5cm) seam allowance, and press open. Make five total 4½" (11.4cm) leaves.

5. Use the same process to sew four 2½" (6.4cm) tan improv squares to two 6½" (16.5cm) light green squares to make two 6½" (16.5cm) leaves.

Make the Blocks

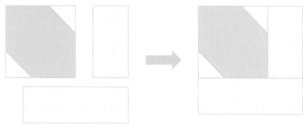

6. Lay out a 4½" (11.4cm) leaf unit, a 2½" x 4½" (6.4 x 11.4cm) tan improv rectangle, and a 2½" x 6½" (6.4 x 16.5cm) tan improv rectangle, with the rectangles arranged around the pointed corner of the leaf as shown. Join the pieces together to complete the leaf block. Make four total leaf blocks.

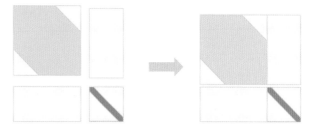

7. Arrange the remaining 4½" (11.4cm) leaf unit, two 2½" x 4½" (6.4 x 11.4cm) tan improv rectangles, and the 2½" (6.4cm) dark green stem block as shown and sew the final leaf block.

Assemble the Quilt Top

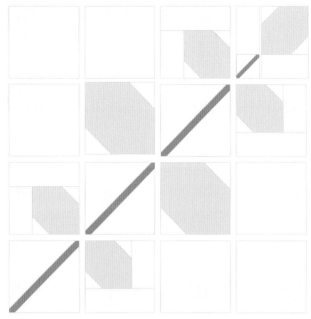

Quilt assembly diagram

8. Referring to the quilt assembly diagram, arrange the blocks and the six 6½" (16.5cm) improv squares into four rows, and sew the rows together to complete the quilt top.

Finish the Quilt

Refer to Finishing Your Quilt on page 112 for instructions on basting, quilting, and binding your quilt.

9. Cut the backing fabric into one piece, measuring 27" x 27" (68.6 x 68.6cm).

10. Layer the backing, batting, and quilt top and baste the layers together. Hand- or machine-quilt as desired. The leaves in the Botanics quilt are outlined and given quilted veins. The background of the quilt is stippled, which creates a denser texture, allowing the leaves to really stand out.

11. Use the 2½" (6.4cm)–wide tan strips to make the binding, then attach it to the quilt.

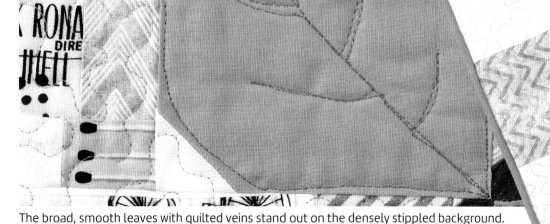

Backing fabric and binding on the finished quilt.

The broad, smooth leaves with quilted veins stand out on the densely stippled background.

Face the Sun

Where I live, there is a local park that plants a giant field of sunflowers every year, and in late summer, the whole city waits for them to bloom. Once the flowers open, families flock to take pictures or just to admire their beauty. A single sunflower takes center stage in this quilt, and the improv piecing makes a great backdrop.

> **Color notes:** Two shades of yellow give the petals in this sunflower some dimension, and the flower really pops against the improv piecing. With so many shades of green in the background, it's easy to imagine this sunflower standing tall in a field.

MATERIALS

With the exception of improv pieces, yardage is based on 42" (106.7cm)–wide fabric.

- One improv piece, 12" x 22" (30.5 x 55.9cm), pieced from assorted green scraps for block and border
- ¼ yard (22.9cm) light yellow fabric for block (Robert Kaufman Fabrics' Kona® Cotton in Sunflower is shown)
- ¼ yard (22.9cm) dark yellow fabric for block (Robert Kaufman Fabrics' Kona® Cotton in Corn Yellow is shown)
- ¼ yard (22.9cm) or one square 5½" (14cm) dark brown for the center of the block (Robert Kaufman Fabrics' Kona® Cotton in Chestnut is shown)
- ¼ yard (22.9cm) fabric for binding, or refer to page 117 to create a scrappy pieced binding measuring 78" (198.1cm)
- ⅔ yard (61cm) fabric for backing, or backing measuring 22" x 22" (55.9 x 55.9cm)
- 22" x 22" (55.9 x 55.9cm) piece of batting

CUTTING

All measurements include ¼" (0.5cm) seam allowances.

From the green improv piece, cut:
- Four squares, 5" (12.7cm)
- Four squares, 3" (7.6cm)
- Four rectangles, 2" x 8" (5.1 x 20.3cm)
- Four rectangles, 2" x 9½" (5.1 x 24.1cm)

From the light yellow fabric, cut:
- Two squares, 5" (12.7cm)
- Four rectangles, 3" x 5½" (7.6 x 14cm)
- Four squares, 2" (5.1cm)

From the dark yellow fabric, cut:
- Two squares, 5" (12.7cm)
- Four squares, 3" (7.6cm)

From the brown fabric, cut:
- One square, 5½" (14cm)

For a solid binding, from the binding fabric, cut:
- Two strips, 2½" x 42" (6.4 x 106.7cm), for binding

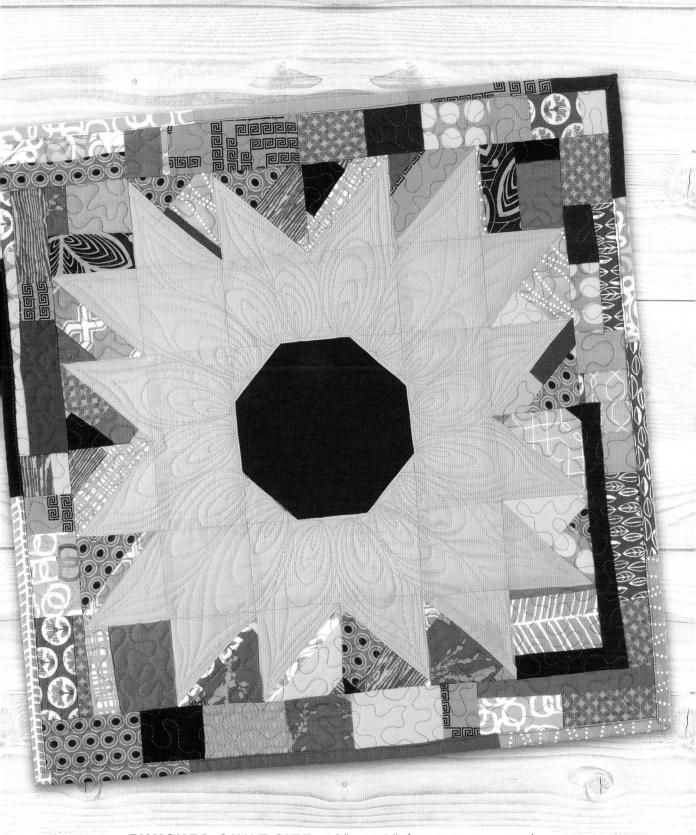

FINISHED QUILT SIZE: 18" X 18" (45.7 X 45.7CM)

Note that improv pieces are represented by solid colors. Refer to page 9 for corner-to-corner sewing methods.

Make the Half-Square Triangles (HSTs)

1. Place one 5" (12.7cm) improv square on one 5" (12.7cm) light yellow square, right sides together. Sew a ¼" (0.5cm) seam around all four edges.

2. Cut the sewn squares twice diagonally from corner to corner and press open to yield four HST units. Trim each HST to 3" (7.6cm) if necessary.

3. Repeat this process to make all remaining HSTs, pairing one 5" (12.7cm) light yellow square and two 5" (12.7cm) dark yellow squares with the three remaining 5" (12.7) improv squares to yield sixteen total HSTs.

Make the Block

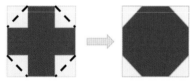

4. Place a 2" (5.1cm) light yellow square on the corner of the 5½" (14cm) brown square, right sides together, and sew from corner to corner. Trim the excess fabric, leaving ¼" (0.5cm) seam allowance.

5. Repeat this process on the remaining corners and press open to yield the center of the block.

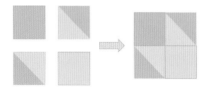

6. Lay out one 3" (7.6cm) green improv square, one 3" (7.6cm) dark yellow square, and two dark yellow HSTs as shown. Sew the pieces and press to complete one corner unit. Make four total corner units.

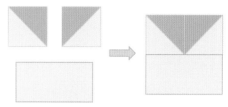

7. Lay out two light yellow HSTs and one 3" x 5½" (7.6 x 14cm) light yellow rectangle as shown. Sew the pieces and press to complete one side unit. Make four total side units.

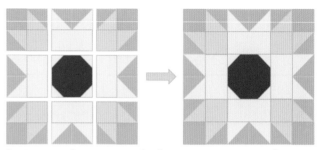

8. Lay out the center unit, four corner units, and four side units into rows as shown, then sew the rows together to complete the block.

Assemble the Quilt Top

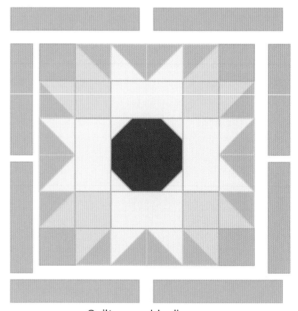

Quilt assembly diagram

9. Referring to the quilt assembly diagram, sew two 2" x 8" (5.1 x 20.3cm) green improv rectangles end to end to create one green improv rectangle measuring 2" x 15½" (5.1 x 39.4cm). Sew the border to the right side of the quilt. Repeat this process to make the border for the left side of the quilt.

10. Referring to the quilt assembly diagram, sew two 2" x 9½" (5.1 x 24.1cm) green improv rectangles end to end to create one green improv rectangle measuring 2" x 18½" (5.1 x 47cm). Sew the border to the top of the quilt. Repeat this process to make the border for the bottom of the quilt.

Because you're sewing narrow strips, piecing the borders with smaller rectangles gives a little extra variety to the improv.

Finish the Quilt

Refer to Finishing Your Quilt on page 112 for instructions on basting, quilting, and binding your quilt.

11. Cut the backing fabric into one piece measuring 22" x 22" (55.9 x 55.9cm).

12. Layer the backing, batting, and quilt top and baste the layers together. Hand- or machine-quilt as desired. The Face the Sun quilt is quilted with pebble quilting in the center, giving the look of seeds, petal quilting on the light and dark yellow areas, and stippling on the green improv background.

13. Use the 2½" (6.4cm)–wide strips of binding fabric or scraps to make the binding and then attach it to the quilt. The green scrappy binding blends into the improv background, allowing the binding to disappear into the quilt.

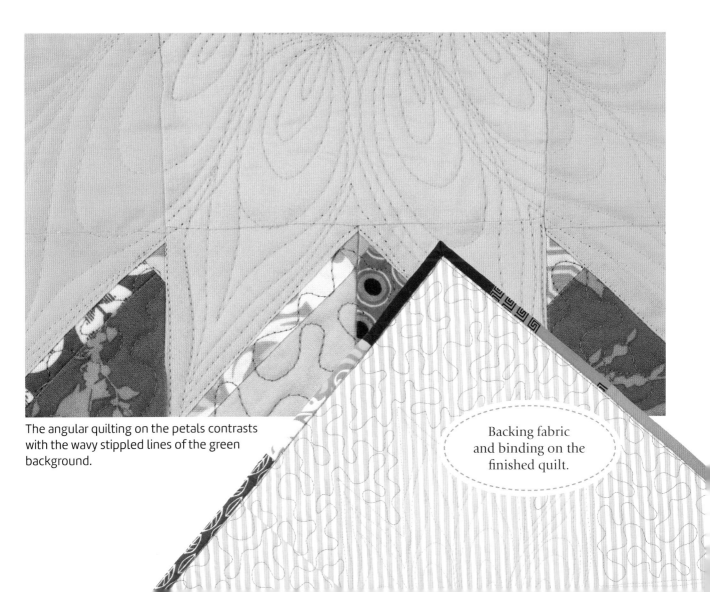

The angular quilting on the petals contrasts with the wavy stippled lines of the green background.

Backing fabric and binding on the finished quilt.

Full Spectrum

Oh, how I love a rainbow! Something about the way one color gradually leads to the next is absolutely magical—and a rainbow created from scraps? Even better. This single-block color wheel is bright and cheerful, and with larger pieces within the block, it makes a bold statement.

> **Color notes:** With only a small improv piece of each color needed, this is a great project for some smaller scraps.

MATERIALS

With the exception of improv pieces, yardage is based on 42" (106.7cm)–wide fabric.

- Four improv pieces, 7" x 7" (17.8 x 17.8cm), pieced from assorted scraps for block; one in each of the following colors: red, yellow, aqua, and purple
- Four improv pieces, 7" x 11" (17.8 x 27.9cm), pieced from assorted scraps for block; one in each of the following colors: orange, green, blue, and pink
- ¼ yard (22.9cm) solid white fabric for block
- ¼ yard (22.9cm) black fabric for binding
- ⅔ yard (61cm) fabric for backing, or backing measuring 22" x 22" (55.9 x 55.9cm)
- 22" x 22" (55.9 x 55.9cm) piece of batting
- Triangle-in-a-square ruler set, such as Tri-Recs

CUTTING

All measurements include ¼" (0.5cm) seam allowances. See Triangle-in-a-Square Blocks on page 10 for instructions on cutting the triangles and triangle side units. When cutting the triangle side units, if your white fabric is a print, keep the fabric folded in half, right sides together, and cut two mirror-image side triangles at the same time.

From each of the red, yellow, aqua, and purple improv pieces, cut:
- One triangle, 6½" (16.5cm)

From each of the orange, green, blue, and pink improv pieces, cut:
- Five squares, 3½" (8.9cm)

From the white background fabric, cut:
- One strip, 7" x 42" (17.8 x 106.7cm); subcut:
  - Four squares, 3½" (8.9cm)
  - Eight triangle side units, 6½" (16.5cm)
  - One square, 6½" (16.5cm)
  - Four rectangles, 3½" x 6½" (8.9 x 16.5cm)

From the binding fabric, cut:
- Two strips, 2½" x 42" (6.4 x 106.7cm), for binding

FINISHED QUILT SIZE: 18" X 18" (45.7 X 45.7CM)

Note that improv pieces are represented by solid colors. Refer to page 9 for corner-to-corner sewing methods.

Make the Side Units

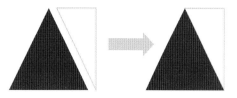

1. Sew a 6½" (16.5cm) white side triangle to the 6½" (16.5cm) red improv triangle and press open.

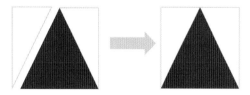

2. Sew a second 6½" (16.5cm) white side triangle to the opposite side of the red improv triangle and press open to make one complete triangle-in-a-square unit. Trim to 6½" (16.5cm) if necessary. Make one triangle-in-a-square unit for each color: red, yellow, aqua, and purple.

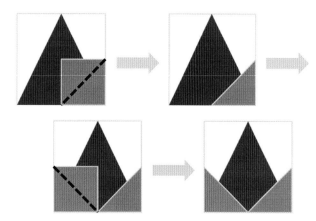

3. Place a 3½" (8.9cm) orange improv square on the bottom right corner of the red improv triangle and sew from corner to corner. Trim the excess fabric, leaving ¼" (0.5cm) seam allowance, and press open. Then sew a 3½" (8.9cm) pink improv square to the bottom left corner of the red improv triangle and press open.

4. Use the process described in step 3 to sew an orange improv square and a green improv square to the corners of the yellow triangle, a green improv square and a blue improv square to the corners of the aqua triangle, and a blue improv square and a pink improv square to the corners of the purple triangle. When you have completed steps 3 and 4, you will have four total side units.

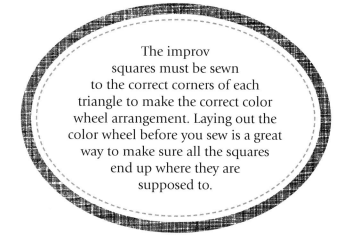

The improv squares must be sewn to the correct corners of each triangle to make the correct color wheel arrangement. Laying out the color wheel before you sew is a great way to make sure all the squares end up where they are supposed to.

Make the Corner Units

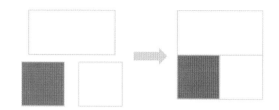

5. Lay out a 3½" (8.9cm) orange improv square, a 3½" (8.9cm) white square, and a 3½" x 6½" (8.9 x 16.5cm) white rectangle as shown and then join the pieces together.

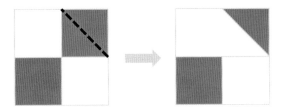

6. Place a 3½" (8.9cm) orange improv square on the top right corner of the unit and sew corner to corner. Trim the excess fabric, leaving ¼" (0.5cm) seam allowance, and press open to make the corner unit. Make four total corner units in this way, one for each color: orange, green, blue, and pink.

Make the Center Unit

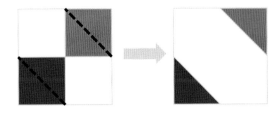

7. Place 3½" (8.9cm) orange and blue improv squares on opposite corners of the 6½" (16.5cm) white square and sew from corner to corner. Trim the excess fabric, leaving ¼" (0.5cm) seam allowance, and press open.

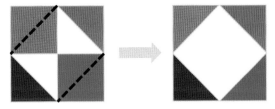

8. Use the same process as in step 7 to sew 3½" (8.9cm) pink and green improv squares to the remaining two corners with the color placement shown above. Trim the excess fabric, leaving ¼" (0.5cm) seam allowance, and press open to complete the center unit.

Assemble the Quilt Top

Quilt assembly diagram

9. Referring to the quilt assembly diagram, arrange the center unit, side units, and corner units into three rows. Sew the rows together to complete the quilt top.

Finish the Quilt

Refer to Finishing Your Quilt on page 112 for instructions on basting, quilting, and binding your quilt.

10. Cut the backing fabric into one piece, measuring 22" x 22" (55.9 x 55.9cm).

11. Layer the backing, batting, and quilt top and baste the layers together. Hand- or machine-quilt as desired. Full Spectrum is quilted with a flower in the center and petal details within each color. The white background is filled with lines that echo the shape of the block.

12. Use the black 2½" (6.4cm)–wide strips to make the binding, then attach it to the quilt.

Backing fabric and binding on the finished quilt.

CHAPTER 3

Simple Shapes

Because improv piecing adds so much texture and dimension, it elevates even the most basic designs into something special. By pairing improv piecing with a clever layout, simple becomes spectacular. Though the quilts in this section are constructed with easy blocks, they are anything but basic!

Prismatic

When I was a child, I thought a prism hanging in a window was one of the neatest things. Actually, I still do! I love the way that prisms catch the light and make rainbows on the wall. The blocks in this quilt are reminiscent of hanging prisms, and they are so much fun to make.

> **Color notes:** Cool shades of purple, blue, and teal take center stage in this quilt. I wanted the quilt to be decidedly on the cool side of the color spectrum, so I left out my warmer red–purple scraps. The bright white background creates a fresh, clean backdrop, which allows these cool colors to really pop.

MATERIALS

With the exception of improv pieces, yardage is based on 42" (106.7cm)–wide fabric.

- One improv piece, 10" x 12" (25.4 x 30.5cm), pieced from assorted purple scraps for blocks
- One improv piece, 10" x 12" (25.4 x 30.5cm), pieced from assorted blue scraps for blocks
- One improv piece, 10" x 12" (25.4 x 30.5cm), pieced from assorted teal/aqua scraps for blocks
- ⅔ yard (61cm) white fabric for blocks and background (Robert Kaufman Fabrics' Kona® Cotton in White is shown)
- ½ yard (45.7cm) navy blue fabric for binding
- ⅔ yard (61cm) fabric for backing, or backing measuring 24" x 28" (30.5 x 71.1cm)
- 24" x 28" (30.5 x 71.1cm) piece of batting

CUTTING

All measurements include ¼" seam allowances.

From the purple, teal/aqua, and blue improv pieces, cut from each:

- Four rectangles, 2½" x 4½" (6.4 x 11.4cm)
- Four rectangles, 2" x 3½" (5.1 x 8.9cm)
- Four rectangles, 1½" x 2½" (3.8 x 6.4cm)

From the white background fabric, cut:

- Two strips, 2½" x 42" (6.4 x 106.7cm); subcut:
  - Twenty-four squares, 2½" (6.4cm), yields eight extra
- Two strips, 2" x 42" (5.1 x 106.7cm); subcut:
  - Twenty-four squares, 2" (5.1cm)
  - Twenty-four rectangles, 1" x 2" (2.5 x 5.1cm)
- Two strips, 1½" x 42" (3.8 x 106.7cm); subcut:
  - Forty-eight squares, 1½" (3.8cm), yields eight extra
- Three strips, 2½" x 42" (6.4 x 106.7cm); subcut:
  - Three rectangles, 2½" x 24½" (6.4 x 62.2cm), for sashing
  - Six rectangles, 2½" x 4½" (6.4 x 11.4cm), for sashing
- One strip, 3½" x 42" (8.9 x 106.7cm); subcut:
  - 1 rectangle, 2½" x 24½" (6.4 x 62.2cm), for sashing
  - 2 rectangles, 3½" x 4½" (8.9 x 11.4cm), for sashing

From the navy blue fabric, cut:

- Three strips, 2½" x 42" (6.4 x 106.7cm), for binding

FINISHED QUILT SIZE: 20" X 24" (50.8 X 61CM)

Note that improv pieces are represented by solid colors. Refer to page 9 for corner-to-corner sewing methods.

Make the Flying Geese

1. Place a 2½" (6.4cm) white square on the corner of a 2½" x 4½" (6.4 x 11.4cm) purple improv rectangle, right sides together, and sew from corner to corner. Trim the excess fabric, leaving ¼" (0.5cm) seam allowance, and press open.

2. Sew a second 2½" (6.4cm) white square to the adjoining corner of the purple rectangle. Trim the excess fabric, leaving ¼" seam allowance, and press open to make one Flying Geese unit. Make four 2½" x 4½" (6.4 x 11.4cm) Flying Geese for each color: purple, blue, and teal.

3. Use the same process as in step 2 to sew 2" (5.1cm) white squares to the corners of the 2" x 3½" (5.1 x 8.9cm) purple, blue, and teal improv rectangles to make four 2" x 3½" (5.1 x 8.9cm) Flying Geese units for each color: purple, blue, and teal.

4. Use the same process to sew 1½" (3.8cm) white squares to the corners of the 1½" x 2½" (3.8 x 6.4cm) purple, blue, and teal improv rectangles to make four 1½" x 2½" (3.8 x 6.4cm) Flying Geese units for each color: purple, blue, and teal.

Make the Blocks

5. Sew a 1½" (3.8cm) white square to each side of a 1½" x 2½" (3.8 x 6.4cm) purple improv Flying Geese unit.

6. Sew a 1" x 2" (2.5 x 5.1cm) rectangle to each side of a 2" x 3½" (5.1 x 8.9cm) purple Flying Geese unit.

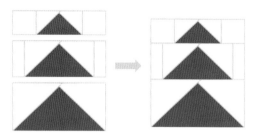

7. Lay out a 2½" x 4½" (6.4 x 11.4cm) purple Flying Geese unit plus the two units created in steps 5 and 6 as shown and join the pieces together to make the block. Make four total blocks for each color: purple, blue, and teal.

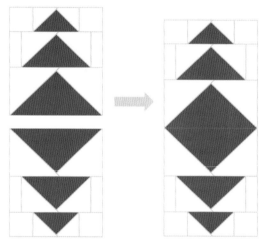

8. Arrange two purple blocks so that the Flying Geese are pointing outward, then sew them together end-to-end to make a purple block set. Repeat this process to make a second purple block set, two teal block sets, and one blue block set. Leave the remaining two blue blocks separate.

Assemble the Quilt Top

9. Referring to the quilt assembly diagram, arrange the block sets, the two blue blocks, and the sashing pieces into columns and sew the columns together to complete the quilt top. In the first and third columns, sew a 2½" x 4½" (6.4 x 11.4cm) white rectangle between the blocks and on the top and bottom of each column. In the center column, sew the 3½" x 4½" (8.9 x 11.4cm) white rectangles between the blocks. Note: The points of the Flying Geese in the center column's blue blocks should point inward.

Finish the Quilt

Refer to Finishing Your Quilt on page 112 for instructions on basting, quilting, and binding your quilt.

10. Cut the backing fabric into one piece, measuring 24" x 28" (61 x 71.1cm).

11. Layer the backing, batting, and quilt top and baste the layers together. Hand- or machine-quilt as desired. Prismatic is quilted with an all-over design using dense, wavy lines, which adds to the hanging look of the blocks in the quilt.

12. Use the 2½" (6.4cm)–wide navy blue strips to make the binding, then attach it to the quilt.

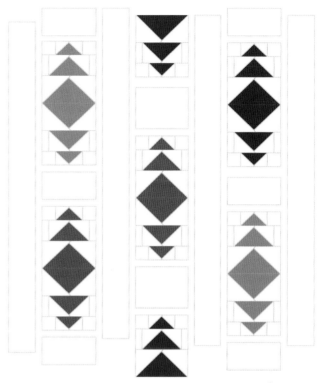

Quilt assembly diagram

Backing fabric and binding on the finished quilt.

Quilted wavy lines accent the entire design.

Downpour

As far as I'm concerned, nature is an inexhaustible source of inspiration. There is beauty to be found in plants and flowers when the weather is sunny, but I find a soaking rain to be beautiful as well. Plus, when the weather is stormy, it's the perfect time to stay inside and create something fun!

Color notes: The raindrops in the Downpour quilt sparkle with aqua scraps. Most of the scraps are in light and medium shades, but just a few darker scraps are thrown in for depth. The background is a super soft blue-gray—a spot-on match for a cloudy day.

MATERIALS

With the exception of improv pieces, yardage is based on 42" (106.7cm)–wide fabric.
- One improv piece, 14" x 15" (35.6 x 38.1cm), pieced from assorted aqua scraps for blocks
- ½ yard (45.7cm) solid gray fabric for blocks and background (Robert Kaufman Fabrics' Kona® Cotton in Fog is shown)
- ¼ yard (22.9cm) aqua fabric for binding
- ⅔ yard fabric for backing, or backing measuring 24" x 24" (61 x 61cm)
- 24" x 24" piece of batting (61 x 61cm)
- Triangle-in-a-square ruler set, such as Tri-Recs

CUTTING

All measurements include ¼" (0.5cm) seam allowances.
See Triangle-in-a-Square Blocks on page 10 for instructions on cutting the triangles and triangle side units. When cutting the triangle side units, if you are using a print fabric in the background, keep the fabric folded in half, right sides together, and cut two mirror-image side triangles at the same time.

From the aqua improv piece, cut:
- One triangle, 5½" (14cm)
- One square, 5½" (14cm)
- Two triangles, 4½" (11.4cm)
- Two squares, 4½" (11.4cm)
- Two triangles, 3½" (8.9cm)
- Two squares, 3½" (8.9cm)

From the gray fabric, cut:
- One strip, 6½" x 42" (16.5 x 106.7cm), subcut:
  - One rectangle, 6½" x 8½" (16.5 x 21.6cm)
  - One rectangle 4½" x 6½" (11.4 x 16.5cm)
  - One rectangle, 1½" x 6½" (3.8 x 16.5cm)
  - Two squares, 5½" (14cm)
  - One rectangle 3½" x 10½" (8.9 x 26.7cm)

- One strip, 2½" x 42" (6.4 x 106.7cm); subcut:
  - Two rectangles 2½" x 10½" (6.4 x 26.7cm)
  - Two rectangles 2½" x 8½" (6.4 x 21.6cm)
- One strip, 2½" x 42" (6.4 x 106.7cm); subcut:
  - Two rectangles 2½" x 3½" (6.4 x 8.9cm)
  - One rectangle 2½" x 4½" (6.4 x 11.4cm)
  - Two squares, 2½" (6.4cm)
  - Four squares, 2" (5.1cm)
  - Four squares, 1½" (3.8cm)
- One strip, 5½" x 42" (14 x 106.7cm); subcut:
  - Two triangle sides, 5½" (14cm)
  - Four triangle sides, 4½" (11.4cm)
  - Four triangle sides, 3½" (8.9cm)

From the binding fabric, cut:
- Three strips, 2½" x 42" (6.4 x 106.7cm), for binding

FINISHED QUILT SIZE: 20" X 20" (50.8 X 50.8CM)

Note that improv pieces are represented by solid colors. Refer to page 9 for corner-to-corner sewing methods.

Make the Raindrop Blocks

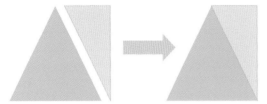

1. Sew a 5½" (14cm) gray side triangle to the side of a 5½" (14cm) aqua improv triangle and press open.

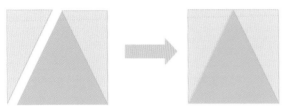

2. Sew a second 5½" (14cm) side triangle to the opposite side of the triangle and press open to make one complete triangle-in-a-square unit measuring 5½" (14cm).

3. In the same manner as steps 1 and 2, sew the 4½" (11.4cm) side triangles to the 4½" (11.4cm) aqua triangles to make two 4½" (11.4cm) triangle-in-a-square units. Then use the same process to sew the 3½" (8.9cm) side triangles to the 3½" (8.9cm) aqua triangles to make two 3½" (8.9cm) triangle-in-a-square units.

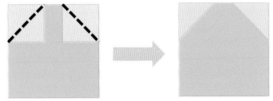

4. Place two 2½" (6.4cm) gray squares on the corners of a 5½" (14cm) aqua improv square, right sides together, and sew from corner to corner. Trim the excess fabric, leaving ¼" (0.5cm) seam allowance, and press open to yield one round unit.

5. In the same manner as step 4, sew two 2" (5.1cm) gray squares to the corners of each 4½" (11.4cm) aqua square to make two round units, each measuring 4½" (11.4cm). Do the same with the 1½" (3.8cm) gray squares, sewing two to the corners of each 3½" (8.9cm) aqua square to make two round units, each measuring 3½" (8.9cm).

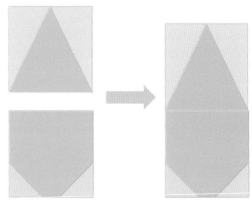

6. Arrange the 5½" (14cm) triangle-in-a-square unit and the 5½" (14cm) round unit as shown, then sew them together to make one 5½" (14cm) raindrop block. Do the same with the pieces you made in steps 3 and 5 to make two 4½" (11.4cm) raindrop blocks and two 3½" (8.9cm) raindrop blocks.

Sew the Quilt Sections

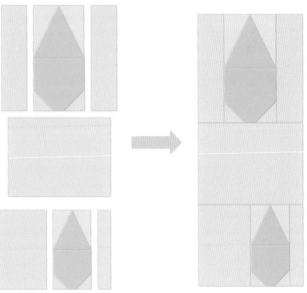

7. Lay out the pieces for section A into three rows as shown, then join the pieces together to make the section.

Section A requires:
- One raindrop block, 4½" (11.4cm)
- One raindrop block, 3½" (8.9cm)
- Two gray rectangles, 2½" x 8½" (6.4 x 21.6cm)
- One gray rectangle 6½" x 8½" (16.5 x 21.6cm)
- One gray rectangle, 4½" x 6½" (11.4 x 16.5cm)
- One gray rectangle, 1½" x 6½" (3.8 x 16.5cm)

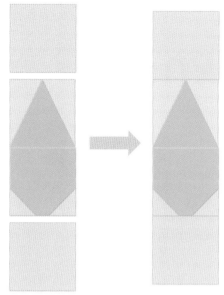

8. Lay out the pieces for section B as shown, then join the pieces together to make the section.

Section B requires:
- One raindrop block, 5½" (14cm)
- Two gray squares, 5½" (14cm)

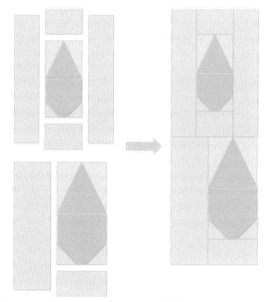

9. Lay out the pieces for section C in two parts as shown, then join the pieces to make the section.

Section C requires:
- One raindrop block, 4½" (11.4cm)
- One raindrop block, 3½" (8.9cm)
- Two gray rectangles, 2½" x 10½" (6.4 x 26.7cm)
- One gray rectangle 3½" x 10½" (8.9 x 26.7cm)
- Two gray rectangles, 2½" x 3½" (6.4 x 8.9cm)
- One gray rectangle, 2½" x 4½" (6.4 x 11.4cm)

Assemble the Quilt Top

Quilt assembly diagram

10. Refer to the quilt assembly diagram to arrange sections A, B, and C in order, then sew the sections together to complete the quilt top.

Finish the Quilt

Refer to Finishing Your Quilt on page 112 for instructions on basting, quilting, and binding your quilt.

11. Cut the backing fabric into one piece, measuring 24" x 24" (61 x 61cm).

12. Layer the backing, batting, and quilt top and baste the layers together. Hand- or machine-quilt as desired. Downpour is quilted with vertical wavy lines to enhance the falling rain effect.

13. Use the 2½" (6.4cm)–wide aqua strips to make the binding, then attach it to the quilt.

Backing fabric and binding on the finished quilt.

Funkytown

On pretty evenings, my husband and I enjoy strolling through our neighborhood. During our walks, we love to discuss the architecture, landscapes, and colors of homes around us, and we marvel at the details that we miss when driving by. There are a few houses that we especially love because they are so interesting, and they were the inspiration for this quilt. Funkytown imagines a whole neighborhood of fun, colorful houses!

Color notes: Don't be afraid to mix solids, prints, and improv in a single quilt; they all play together nicely in Funkytown. The scrappy improv houses each have a contrasting solid front door, and the consistent design of the rooftops keeps the quilt from looking too busy. The whisper–soft blue background looks like a perfect cloudless day and allows the other colors to pop.

MATERIALS
With the exception of improv pieces, yardage is based on 42" (106.7cm)–wide fabric.
- One improv piece, 10" x 23" (25.4 x 58.4cm) pieced from assorted multi-colored scraps, for house blocks
- One improv piece, 7" x 11" (17.8 x 27.9cm) pieced from assorted green scraps for tree blocks
- ⅔ yard (61cm) light blue fabric for background (Robert Kaufman Fabrics' Kona® Cotton in Cloud is shown)
- ⅛ yard (11.4cm) black print fabric for roofs of house blocks
- ⅛ yard (11.4cm) solid brown fabric for trunks of tree blocks (Robert Kaufman Fabrics' Kona® Cotton in Chestnut is shown)
- Ten different solid scrap pieces, 1½" x 2½" (3.8 x 6.4cm), for doors of house blocks
- ½ yard (45.7cm) dark gray print fabric for street sashing and binding
- 1 yard (91.44cm) fabric for backing, or backing measuring 34" x 34" (86.4 x 86.4cm)
- 34" x 34" (86.4 x 86.4cm) piece of batting

CUTTING
All measurements include ¼" (0.5cm) seam allowances.

From the mixed–color improv piece, cut:
- Ten rectangles, 2½" x 4½" (6.4 x 11.4cm)
- Twenty rectangles, 2" x 2½" (5.1 x 6.4cm)

From the green improv piece, cut:
- Six squares, 3½" (8.9cm)

From the black print fabric, cut:
- Ten rectangles, 2½" x 4½" (6.4 x 11.4cm)

From the solid brown fabric, cut:
- Six rectangles, 1½" x 3½" (3.8 x 8.9cm)

From the light blue background fabric, cut:
- One strip, 6½" x 42" (16.5 x 106.7cm); subcut:
  - Fourteen rectangles, 2½" x 6½" (6.4 x 16.5cm), yields two extra

- One strip, 6½" x 42" (16.5 x 106.7cm); subcut:
  - Two rectangles, 6½" x 9½" (16.5 x 24.1cm)
  - Two rectangles, 6½" x 8½" (16.5 x 21.6cm)
- Two strips, 2½" x 42" (6.4 x 106.7cm); subcut:
  - Three rectangles, 2½" x 5½" (6.4 x 14cm)
  - Twenty squares, 2½" (6.4cm)
- One strip, 1½" x 42" (3.8 x 106.7cm); subcut:
  - Twelve rectangles, 1½" x 3½" (3.8 x 8.9cm)
- One strip, 1½" x 42" (3.8 x 106.7cm); subcut:
  - Twenty-four squares, 1½" (3.8cm), yields four extra

From the dark gray print fabric, cut:
- Three strips, 2½" x 42" (6.4 x 106.7cm); subcut:
  - Three rectangles, 2½" x 25½" (6.4 x 64.8cm)
  - Four strips, 2½" x 42" (6.4 x 106.7cm) for binding

FINISHED QUILT SIZE: 30" X 30" (76.2 X 76.2CM)

Note that improv pieces are represented by solid colors. Refer to page 9 for corner-to-corner sewing methods.

Make the House Blocks

1. Place a 2½" (6.4cm) blue square on the corner of one 2½" x 4½" (6.4 x 11.4cm) black rectangle, right sides together, and sew from corner to corner. Trim the excess fabric, leaving ¼" (0.5cm) seam allowance, and press open.

2. Repeat on the adjoining corner to yield one roof unit measuring 2½" x 4½" (6.4 x 11.4cm), including seam allowances.

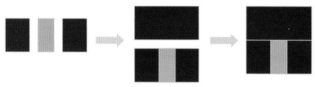

3. Sew a 2" x 2½" (5.1 x 6.4cm) improv rectangle to each side of one contrasting 1½" x 2½" (3.8 x 6.4cm) solid rectangle. Then sew a 2½" x 4½" (6.4 x 11.4cm) improv rectangle to the top to yield one house unit measuring 4½" square (11.4cm), including seam allowances.

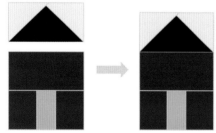

4. Sew the roof unit to the top of the house unit to create one house block measuring 4½" x 6½" (11.4 x 16.5cm), including seam allowances. Repeat this process to make ten house blocks.

Make the Tree Blocks

5. Place a 1½" (3.8cm) blue square on the corner of one 3½" (8.9cm) green improv square, right sides together, and sew from corner to corner. Trim the excess fabric, leaving ¼" (0.5cm) seam allowance, and press open. Repeat this process on the remaining corners to yield one tree unit.

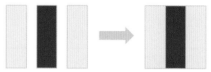

6. Sew a 1½" x 3½" (3.8 x 8.9cm) blue rectangle to each side of one 1½" x 3½" (3.8 x 8.9cm) brown rectangle and press open to yield one trunk unit.

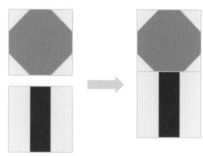

7. Sew the tree unit to the top of the trunk unit to yield one complete tree block measuring 3½" x 6½" (8.9 x 16.5cm). Make six tree blocks.

Assemble the Rows

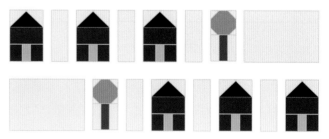

8. Lay out three house blocks, one tree block, three 2½" x 6½" (6.4 x 16.5cm) blue rectangles, and one 6½" x 9½" (16.5 x 24.1cm) rectangle as shown. Join the pieces and press to complete row 1. Then repeat this process but lay out the pieces and sew them together in the reverse order of row 1 as shown; this will be row 4.

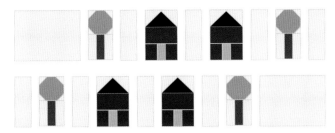

9. Lay out two house blocks, two tree blocks, four 2½" x 6½" (6.4 x 16.5cm) blue rectangles, and one 6½" x 8½" (16.5 x 21.6cm) rectangle as shown. Join the pieces and press to complete row 2. Repeat this process but lay out the pieces and sew them together in the reverse order of row 2 as shown; this will be row 3.

10. Sew a 2½" x 5½" (6.4 x 14cm) blue rectangle to the end of one 2½" x 25½" (6.4 x 64.8cm) dark gray rectangle to make one sashing strip measuring 2½" x 30½" (6.4 x 77.5cm). Repeat this process to make three total sashing strips.

Assemble the Quilt Top

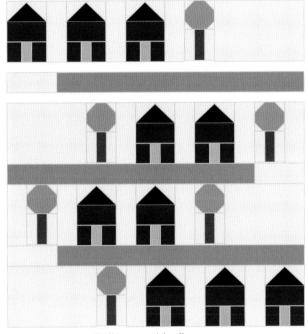

Quilt assembly diagram

11. Refer to the quilt assembly diagram to arrange the four rows of the quilt, then sew the rows together with the sashing strips between the rows. Note that the blue rectangles of the sashing strips should alternate direction.

Finish the Quilt

Refer to Finishing Your Quilt on page 112 for instructions on basting, quilting, and binding your quilt.

12. Cut the backing fabric into one piece, measuring 34" x 34" (86.4 x 86.4cm).

13. Layer the backing, batting, and quilt top and baste the layers together. Hand- or machine-quilt as desired. Because Funkytown contains a mix of prints, solids, and improv, the quilting is a little simpler. An all-over stipple gives the quilt plenty of texture without competing with the patterns.

14. Use the 2½" (6.4cm)–wide dark gray strips to make the binding, then attach it to the quilt.

The simple stippling adds texture to the quilt's many patterns and colors.

Cherub Wings

Cherubs are often depicted in art as beautiful children with wings, and this pair of wings is sure to make a lovely statement wherever it is displayed. Hang this quilt on a wall for an eye-catching focal point or use it as a precious backdrop for photographing your little one.

> **Color notes:** The improv background in this quilt uses every color in the rainbow as well as multi-colored fabrics that can sometimes be difficult to mix with other scraps. The explosion of scraps creates a cheerful quilt, but this quilt would also look stunning made in softer colors for a nursery or in a controlled palette to match the décor of a room.

MATERIALS

With the exception of improv pieces, yardage is based on 42" (106.7cm)–wide fabric.
- Three improv pieces, 11" x 21" (27.9 x 53.3cm), pieced from assorted multi-colored scraps for blocks
- One improv piece, 13" x 18" (33 x 45.7cm), pieced from assorted multi-colored scraps for blocks
- ½ yard (45.7cm) solid white fabric for wings
- ⅓ yard (30.5cm) fabric for binding, or refer to page 117 to create a scrappy pieced binding measuring 126" (320cm)
- 1 yard (91.4cm) fabric for backing, or backing measuring 33" x 34" (83.8 x 86.4cm)
- 33" x 34" (83.8 x 86.4cm) piece of batting

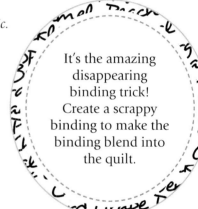

It's the amazing disappearing binding trick! Create a scrappy binding to make the binding blend into the quilt.

CUTTING

All measurements include ¼" (0.5cm) seam allowances.

From each 11" x 21" (27.9 x 53.3cm) improv piece, cut:
- Eighteen squares, 3½" (8.9cm), fifty total, yields four extra

From the 13" x 18" (33 x 45.7cm) improv piece, cut:
- Two rectangles, 3" x 13" (7.6 x 33cm)
- Two rectangles, 3½" x 9" (8.9 x 22.9cm)
- Two rectangles, 1½" x 5" (3.8 x 12.7cm)
- Two rectangles, 2" x 3½" (5.1 x 8.9cm)
- Two rectangles, 2" x 3" (5.1 x 7.6cm)
- Two squares, 1½" (3.8cm)
- Twenty-four squares, 1" (2.5cm), or cut one square, 1" (2.5cm), from each of twenty-four different scrap pieces

From the solid white fabric, cut:
- One strip, 7½" x 42" (19.1 x 106.7cm); subcut:
  - Two rectangles, 7½" x 10½" (19.1 x 26.7cm)
  - Two rectangles, 2" x 11½" (5.1 x 29.2cm)
- One strip, 2" x 42" (5.1 x 106.7cm); subcut:
  - Two rectangles, 2" x 17½" (5.1 x 44.5cm)
- One strip, 2" x 42" (5.1 x 106.7cm); subcut:
  - Two rectangles, 2" x 14½" (5.1 x 36.8cm)
  - Two rectangles, 2" x 5" (5.1 x 12.7cm)
- One strip, 2" x 42" (5.1 x 106.7cm); subcut:
  - Two rectangles, 2" x 9" (5.1 x 22.9cm)
  - Two rectangles, 2" x 6½" (5.1 x 16.5cm)

For a solid binding, from the binding fabric, cut:
- Four strips, 2½" x 42" (6.4 x 106.7cm) for binding

FINISHED QUILT SIZE: 29" X 30" (73.7 X 76.2CM)

Make the Wings

Note that improv pieces are represented by solid colors. Refer to page 9 for corner-to-corner sewing methods. This quilt requires sewing a mirror image of each unit to create wings that face each other. Each step includes directions for sewing one wing unit and then its mirror image in the same step.

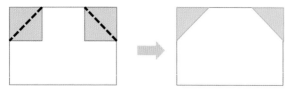

1. Place two 3½" (8.9cm) improv squares on the top corners of a 7½" x 10½" (19.1 x 26.7cm) rectangle, right sides together, and sew from corner to corner. Trim the excess fabric, leaving ¼" (0.5cm) seam allowance, and press open. Make two identical units.

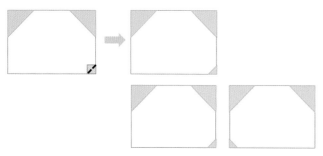

2. Place a 1½" (3.8cm) improv square on the bottom right corner of a 7½" x 10½" (19.1 x 26.7cm) rectangle, right sides together, and sew from corner to corner. Trim the excess fabric, leaving ¼" (0.5cm) seam allowance, and press open. Sew a 1½" (3.8cm) improv square to the bottom left corner of the second 7½" x 10½" (19.1 x 26.7cm) rectangle to make mirror-image units as shown.

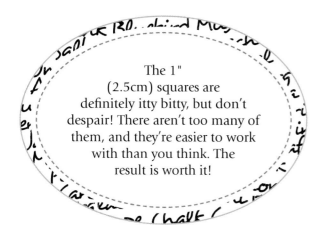

The 1" (2.5cm) squares are definitely itty bitty, but don't despair! There aren't too many of them, and they're easier to work with than you think. The result is worth it!

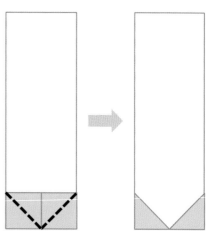

3. Place two 1" (2.5cm) improv squares on the bottom corners of a 2" x 5" (5.1 x 12.7cm) rectangle, right sides together, and sew from corner to corner. Trim the excess fabric, leaving ¼" (0.5cm) seam allowance, and press open. Sew the remaining 1" (2.5cm) squares to the remaining 2" (5.1cm) white strips in the same manner to make the feather units.

Note: Because of the seam allowance, the ends of the feather units will look pointed when the corner squares are sewn on, but they will be rounded when they are pieced with the other quilt blocks.

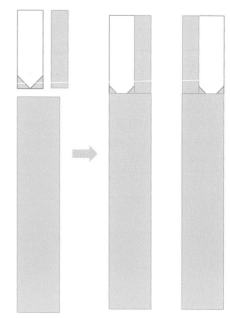

4. Lay out one 2" x 5" (5.1 x 12.7cm) feather unit, one 1½" x 5 (3.8 x 12.7cm) improv rectangle, and one 3" x 13" (7.6 x 33cm) improv rectangle as shown. Join the pieces together to make feather A. Repeat this process to make a mirror image of feather A for the second wing.

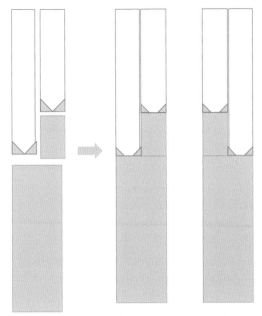

5. Lay out one 2" x 6½" (5.1 x 16.5cm) feather unit, one 2" x 9" (5.1 x 22.9cm) feather unit, one 2" x 3" (5.1 x 7.6cm) improv rectangle, and one 3½" x 9" (8.9 x 22.9cm) improv rectangle as shown. Join the pieces together to make feathers B and C. Repeat this process to make a mirror image of feathers B and C for the second wing.

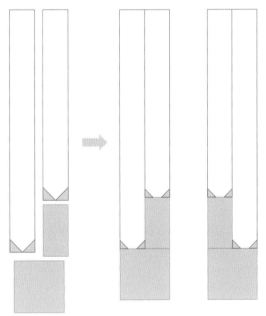

6. Lay out one 2" x 11½" (5.1 x 29.2cm) feather unit, one 2" x 14½" (5.1 x 36.8cm) feather unit, one 2" x 3½" (5.1 x 8.9cm) improv rectangle, and one 3½" (8.9cm) improv square as shown. Join the pieces together to make feathers D and E. Repeat this process to make a mirror image of feathers D and E for the second wing.

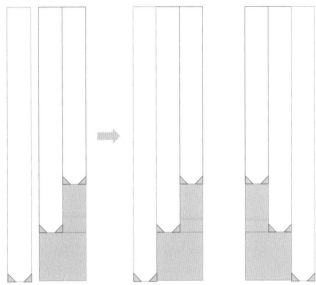

7. Sew the 2" x 17½" (5.1 x 44.5cm) feather unit to the side of feathers D and E as shown. Repeat this process for the second wing, sewing the feather unit in a mirror image as shown.

Assemble the Wings

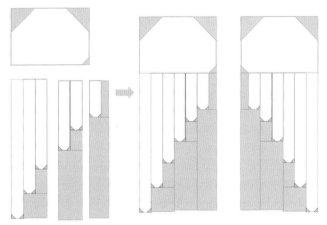

8. Lay out the feather units in order from shortest to longest from the inside of the wing. Sew the feather units together. Then sew the top of the wing onto the feathers as shown, creating two complete mirror-image wings. Each wing should measure 10½" x 24½" (26.7 x 62.2cm), including seam allowances.

Assemble the Quilt Top

9. Sew eight 3½" (8.9cm) improv squares together end-to-end to make one long improv strip, measuring 3½" x 24½" (8.9 x 62.2cm) and press. Make three strips.

10. Sew ten 3½" (8.9cm) improv squares together end-to-end to make one long improv strip, measuring 3½" x 30½" (8.9 x 77.5cm), and press. Trim the strip to 29½" (75cm) long. Repeat the process to make a second strip.

Quilt assembly diagram

11. Refer to the quilt assembly diagram to sew one 24½" (62.2cm) strip between the two wings and two 24½" strips to each side of the quilt top. Then sew a 29½" (75cm) strip to the top and bottom of the quilt top to complete the quilt top.

Finish the Quilt

Refer to Finishing Your Quilt on page 112 for instructions on basting, quilting, and binding your quilt.

12. Cut the backing fabric into one piece, measuring 33" x 34" (83.8 x 86.4cm).

13. Layer the backing, batting, and quilt top and baste the layers together. Hand- or machine-quilt as desired. Cherub Wings is quilted with free-motion feathers on each individual wing to add dimension, and it is filled with denser stippling in the background to give the feathers a puffier texture.

14. Use the 2½" (6.4cm)–wide strips of binding fabric or scraps to make the binding, then attach it to the quilt.

Backing fabric and binding on the finished quilt.

The quilting is intended to give the wings a puffy, airy feel.

Chapel Window

Many cathedrals and churches are known for their beautiful stained glass, with its intricate, awe-inspiring detail work. Stained glass artistry can be found in smaller, less formal churches and chapels as well, and though the patterns may be less ornate, they are no less lovely. The simple yet striking stained glass design in this mini quilt appears to glow against the black background, making it appear lit from within.

Color notes: When I make scrap quilts, I often neglect my solid scraps. I do mix a few of them in with my prints, but I always have a lot of solids left over, and this quilt is a great home for them. Because most stained glass is created with glass pieces in single colors, solid-colored fabrics really give the most realistic stained glass look. However, if you're not a big fan of solid fabrics, try tonal, near-solid colors, which will work equally well. Be sure to choose brighter tones if you want your quilt to really look full of light.

MATERIALS

With the exception of improv pieces, yardage is based on 42" (106.7cm)-wide fabric.
- Two improv pieces, 11" x 21" (27.9 x 53.3cm), pieced from assorted solid scraps for blocks
- Sixteen additional solid scrap pieces in different colors, 1" (2.5cm), for cornerstone squares
- ⅝ yard (57.2cm) solid black fabric for blocks, background, and binding
- ¾ yard (68.6cm) fabric for backing, or backing measuring 27" x 27" (68.6 x 68.6cm)
- 27" x 27" (68.6 x 68.6cm) piece of batting

CUTTING

All measurements include ¼" (0.5cm) seam allowances.

From each improv piece, cut:
- Eighteen squares, 3½" (8.9cm), thirty-six total

From the additional solid scrap pieces, cut:
- Sixteen squares, 1" (2.5cm) each, from sixteen different pieces

From the black fabric, cut:
- Two strips, 2" x 42" (5.1 x 106.7cm); subcut:
  - Thirty-six squares, 2" (5.1cm), yields four extra
- One strip, 7" x 42" (17.8 x 106.7cm); subcut:
  - Thirty-three rectangles, 1"x 7" (2.5 x 17.8cm)
  - Fourteen rectangles, 1" x 3½" (2.5 x 8.9cm)
- One strip, 1" x 42" (2.5 x 106.7cm), subcut:
  - Four rectangles, 1" x 3½" (2.5 x 8.9cm), eighteen total
  - Three strips, 2½" x 42" (6.4 x 106.7cm), for binding

Note that improv blocks are represented by solid colors. Refer to page 9 for corner-to-corner sewing methods.

Make the Blocks

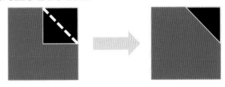

1. Place a 2" (5.1cm) black square on the corner of a 3½" (8.9cm) improv square, right sides together, and sew from corner to corner. Trim the excess fabric, leaving ¼" (0.5cm) seam allowance, and press open to make an improv block unit. Make four units.

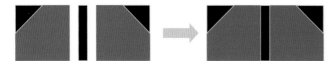

2. Sew an improv block unit to each side of a 1" x 3½" (2.5 x 8.9cm) black rectangle to complete half of the block. Note that the black corners should be arranged at the top of the block, pointing toward the outside, as shown. Make two identical block halves.

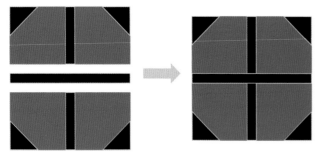

3. Arrange the block halves as shown and sew a 1" x 7" (2.5 x 17.8cm) black rectangle between the two halves to complete the block. Make nine blocks.

Make the Sashing

4. Lay out four 1" (2.5cm) colored squares and three 1" x 7" (2.5 x 17.8cm) black rectangles in an alternating pattern and join them together end-to-end as shown to make a sashing strip. Begin and end the sashing strip with a colored square. Make four total sashing strips.

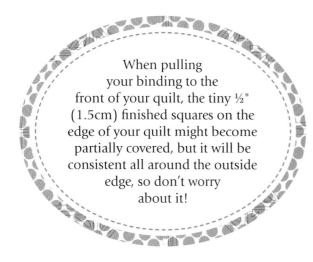

When pulling your binding to the front of your quilt, the tiny ½" (1.5cm) finished squares on the edge of your quilt might become partially covered, but it will be consistent all around the outside edge, so don't worry about it!

Assemble the Quilt Top

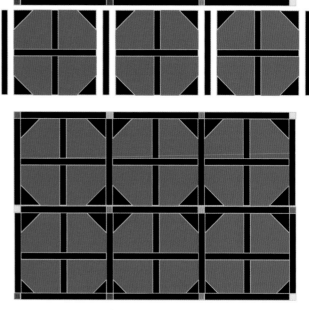

Quilt assembly diagram

5. Refer to the quilt assembly diagram to lay out the blocks and 1" x 7" (2.5 x 17.8cm) black rectangles into three rows as shown, then join the blocks and rectangles together to make the rows.

6. Sew the sashing strips between each row and to the top and bottom of the quilt to complete the quilt top.

Finish the Quilt

Refer to page 112 for instructions on basting, quilting, and binding your quilt.

7. Cut the backing fabric into one piece, measuring 27" x 27" (68.6 x 68.6cm).

8. Layer the backing, batting, and quilt top and baste the layers together. Hand- or machine-quilt as desired. Chapel Window is quilted with dense lines to echo the design.

9. Use the 2½" (6.4cm)–wide black strips to make the binding, then attach it to the quilt.

FINISHED QUILT SIZE: 22½" X 22½" (57.2 X 57.2CM)

CHAPTER 4

Seasonal Sensations

I love decorating my home for Christmas. I cover every available surface with some sort of Christmas cheer. During the rest of the year, though, I definitely lack that same gusto. Still, it's nice to have an easy way to give my home a little nod to the season, and mini quilts that can be changed quickly are a wonderful solution.

Winter Frost

After the hustle and bustle of the holidays are over, and all of the decorations are put away, I always think my home looks a bit bare. Although it's nice to reclaim my house from the holidays, I still want a little seasonal cheer. This snowflake quilt is a perfect pick-me-up to fight off the doldrums of winter.

> **Color notes:** Winter Frost uses tone-on-tone white, solid white and cream, and metallic silver scraps to create a cool, icy look against an aqua background. If you don't have metallic silver scraps, use a few soft gray scraps to create the same look. The aqua background in this quilt is a crosshatch print rather than a solid, which adds extra texture.

MATERIALS

With the exception of improv pieces, yardage is based on 42" (106.7cm)–wide fabric.
- Two improv pieces, 9" x 21" (22.9 x 53.3cm), each pieced from assorted white, cream, and silver scraps for blocks
- ½ yard (45.7cm) aqua fabric for blocks
- ⅔ yard (61cm) fabric for backing, or backing measuring 24" x 24" (61 x 61cm)
- ¼ yard (22.9cm) metallic silver fabric for binding
- 24" x 24" (61 x 61cm) piece of batting
- Triangle-in-a-square ruler set, such as Tri-Recs

CUTTING

All measurements include ¼" (0.5cm) seam allowances.
See Triangle-in-a-Square Blocks on page 10 for instructions on cutting the triangles and triangle side units. When cutting the triangle side units, if you are using a print fabric in the background, keep the fabric folded in half, right sides together, and cut two mirror-image side triangles at the same time.

From one improv piece, cut:
- Eight rectangles, 2½" x 4½" (6.4 x 11.4cm)
- One square, 4½" (11.4cm)
- Four rectangles, 3" x 4½" (7.6 x 11.4cm)

From one improv piece, cut:
- Four rectangles, 2" x 4½" (5.1 x 11.4cm)
- Four rectangles, 2" x 3" (5.1 x 7.6cm)
- Eight squares, 2½" (6.4cm)
- Four rectangles, 1½" x 2" (3.8 x 5.1cm)
- Eight triangles, 2½" (6.4cm)

From the aqua fabric, cut:
- One strip, 3" x 42" (7.6 x 106.7cm); subcut:
  - Four squares, 3" (7.6cm)
  - Thirty-two squares, 1½" (3.8cm)
- Two strips, 2½" x 42" (6.4 x 106.7cm); subcut:
  - Twenty-four squares, 2½" (6.4cm)
  - Sixteen triangle side units, 2½" (6.4cm)
- One strip, 2" x 42" (5.1 x 106.7cm); subcut:
  - Twenty squares 2" (5.1cm)
- Three strips, 1½" x 42" (3.8 x 106.7cm); subcut:
  - Twenty-four rectangles, 1½" x 4½" (3.8 x 11.4cm), yields three extra

From the silver fabric, cut:
- Two strips, 2½" x 42" (6.4 x 106.7cm) for binding

FINISHED QUILT SIZE: 20" X 20" (50.8 X 50.8CM)

Note that improv pieces are represented by solid colors. Refer to page 9 for corner-to-corner sewing methods.

Make the Blocks

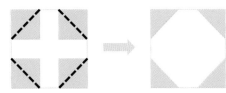

1. Place a 2" (5.1cm) aqua square on the corner of a 4½" (11.4cm) improv square, right sides together, and sew from corner to corner. Trim the excess fabric, leaving ¼" (0.5cm) seam allowance, and press open. Repeat this process on the remaining three corners to make the center unit.

2. Place a 2" (5.1cm) aqua square on the corner of a 2" x 3" (5.1 x 7.6cm) improv rectangle, right sides together, and sew from corner to corner. Trim the excess fabric, leaving ¼" (0.5cm) seam allowance, and press open.

3. Place a 2" (5.1cm) aqua square on the corner of a 2" x 4½" (5.1 x 11.4cm) improv rectangle, right sides together, and sew from corner to corner in the opposite direction. Trim the excess fabric, leaving ¼" (0.5cm) seam allowance, and press open.

4. Lay out the units from steps 2 and 3, plus a 3" (7.6cm) aqua square, and join the pieces together to create one unit A. Make four total unit As.

5. Place a 2½" (6.4cm) aqua square on the corner of a 2½" x 4½" (6.4 x 11.4cm) improv rectangle, right sides together, and sew from corner to corner. Trim the excess fabric, leaving ¼" (0.5cm) seam allowance, and press open.

6. Repeat this process on the adjoining corner to make one Flying Geese unit. Then sew one 1½" x 4½" (3.8 x 11.4cm) aqua rectangle to each side of the Flying Geese unit and press open to create one unit B. Make eight total unit Bs.

7. Place two 1½" (3.8cm) aqua squares on opposite corners of a 2½" (6.4cm) improv square, right sides together, and sew from corner to corner. Trim the excess fabric, leaving ¼" (0.5cm) seam allowance, and press open. Repeat this process to make an identical second unit. Then arrange both units and two 2½" (6.4cm) aqua squares as shown. Join the pieces together to create one unit C. Make four total unit Cs.

8. Place a 1½" (3.8cm) aqua square on the corner of one 3" x 4½" (7.6 x 11.4cm) improv rectangle, right sides together, and sew from corner to corner as shown. Trim the excess fabric, leaving ¼" (0.5cm) seam allowance, and press open. Repeat this process on the remaining three corners.

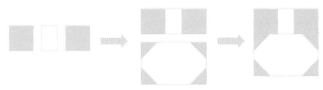

9. Sew a 2" (5.1cm) aqua square to each side of a 1½" x 2" (3.8 x 5.1cm) improv rectangle, then sew it to the top of the unit from step 8 to create one unit D. Make four total unit Ds.

10. Sew an aqua side triangle to a 2½" (6.4cm) improv triangle and press open.

11. Sew a second aqua side triangle to the opposite side of the triangle and press open to yield one complete triangle-in-a-square unit. Make a second identical unit.

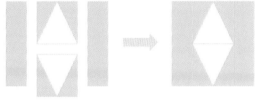

12. Lay out the two triangle-in-a-square units in a diamond shape and two 1½" x 4½" (3.8 x 11.4cm) aqua rectangles as shown, then join the pieces together to make one unit E. Make four total unit Es.

Assemble the Quilt Top

Quilt assembly diagram

13. Refer to the quilt assembly diagram to arrange the units into five rows with five blocks in each row, then sew the rows together as shown.

Finish the Quilt

Refer to Finishing Your Quilt on page 112 for instructions on basting, quilting, and binding your quilt.

14. Cut the backing fabric into one piece, measuring 24" x 24" (61 x 61cm).

15. Layer the backing, batting, and quilt top and baste the layers together. Hand- or machine-quilt as desired. Winter Frost is quilted with swooping lines that spin out from the center in a giant spiral, adding lots of movement to the pattern.

16. Use the silver 2½" (6.4cm)–wide strips to make the binding, then attach it to the quilt.

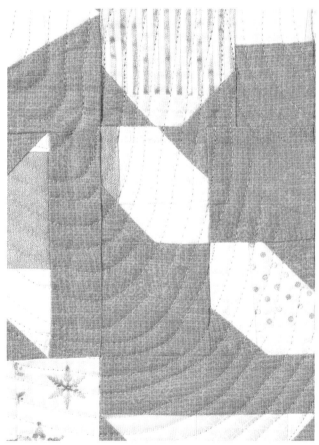

A large, swooping spiral adds lots of movement to the quilt.

Heartstruck

My hubby and I don't go overboard celebrating Valentine's Day, but it is fun to acknowledge just a little bit. This holiday comes during the bleakest part of winter, and a few cheery hearts are fantastic for lifting spirits during the gray days of February. The fun hearts and arrows in this quilt are perfect for a festive Valentine's Day table setting.

> **Color notes:** The hearts in this quilt are sewn with a mix of reds and pinks, and they serve as a great contrast for the many shades of gray in the arrows. A bright white background keeps this quilt light and airy while allowing the reds and pinks to jump right out.

MATERIALS
With the exception of improv pieces, yardage is based on 42" (106.7cm)–wide fabric.
- One improv piece, 12" x 14" (30.5 x 35.6cm), pieced from assorted red and pink scraps for blocks
- One improv piece, 14" x 14" (35.6 x 35.6cm), pieced from assorted gray scraps for blocks
- ⅔ yard (61cm) solid white fabric for blocks and background
- ¼ yard (22.9cm) pink/red fabric for binding
- ¾ yard (68.6cm) fabric for backing, or backing measuring 27" x 27" (68.6 x 68.6cm)
- 27" x 27" (68.6 x 68.6cm) piece of batting
- Triangle-in-a-square ruler set, such as Tri-Recs

CUTTING
All measurements include ¼" (0.5cm) seam allowances.
See Triangle-in-a-Square Blocks on page 10 for instructions on cutting the triangles and triangle side units. When cutting the triangle side units, if you are using a print fabric in the background, keep the fabric folded in half, right sides together, and cut two mirror-image side triangles at the same time.

From the red/pink improv piece, cut:
- Three triangles, 6½" (16.5cm)
- Six rectangles, 2½" x 3½" (6.4 x 8.9cm)

From the gray improv piece, cut:
- Three triangles, 4½" (11.4cm)
- Three squares, 3½" (8.9cm)
- Three rectangles, 1½" x 13½" (3.8 x 34.3cm)

From the solid white background fabric, cut:
- One strip, 6½" x 42" (16.5 x 106.7cm); subcut:
  - Six triangle side units, 6½" (16.5cm)
  - Six triangle side units, 4½" (11.4cm)
  - Three squares, 3½" (8.9cm)
- Three strips, 2½" x 42" (6.4 x 106.7cm); subcut:
  - Six rectangles, 2½" x 17½" (6.4 x 44.5cm)
- Two strips, 2" x 42" (5.1 x 106.7cm); subcut:
  - Six rectangles, 2" x 10½" (5.1 x 26.7cm)
  - Twelve squares, 1½" (3.8cm)
- One strip, 1½" x 42" (3.8 x 106.7cm); subcut:
  - Three rectangles, 1½" x 8½" (3.8 x 21.6cm)

From the binding fabric, cut:
- Three strips, 2½" x 42" (6.4 x 106.7cm), for binding

FINISHED QUILT SIZE: 24" X 24" (61 X 61CM)

Note that improv pieces are represented by solid colors. Refer to page 9 for corner-to-corner sewing methods.

Make the Arrow Blocks

1. Place a 3½" (8.9cm) gray improv square on one 3½" (8.9cm) white square, right sides together. Sew a ¼" (0.5cm) seam around all four edges of the squares.

2. Cut the sewn squares twice diagonally from corner to corner and press open to yield four HSTs. Trim each HST to 2" (5.1cm) if necessary. Repeat this process to make twelve total HSTs, each measuring 2" (5.1cm).

3. Sew one 4½" (11.4cm) white side triangle unit to the side of one 4½" (11.4cm) gray improv triangle and press open.

4. Repeat this process on the opposite side of the triangle and press open to make an arrowhead unit. Trim to 4½" (11.4cm) if necessary. Make three total arrowhead units.

5. Lay out two gray improv HSTs and one 2" x 10½" (5.1 x 26.7cm) white rectangle as shown and join the pieces together end-to-end to create one feather unit. Repeat this process to create a mirror-image feather unit.

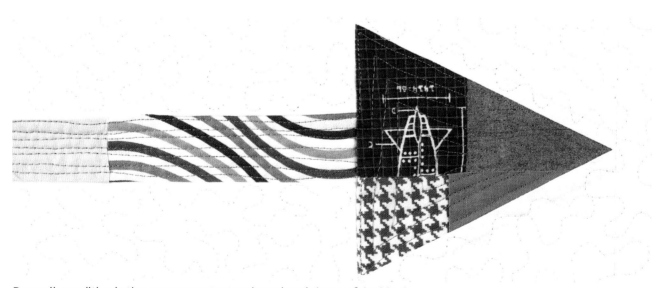

Dense line quilting in the arrow accentuates the pointed shape of the block.

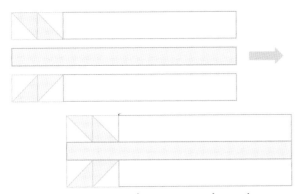

6. Sew one 1½" x 13½" (3.8 x 34.3cm) gray improv rectangle between the two mirror-image feather units to create the body of an arrow.

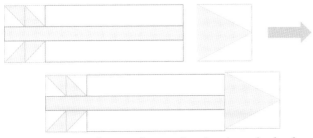

7. Sew one 4½" (11.4cm) arrowhead unit to the body of the arrow with the point facing outward to create an arrow unit.

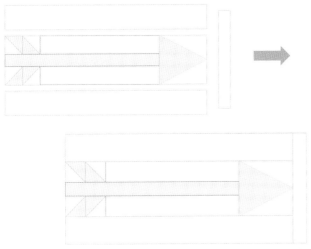

8. Sew one 2½" x 17½" (6.4 x 44.5cm) white rectangle to the top and bottom of the arrow unit. Then sew the 1½" x 8½" (3.8 x 21.6cm) white rectangle to the point of the arrow unit to complete the arrow block. Repeat steps 5–8 to make three total arrow blocks.

Make the Heart Blocks

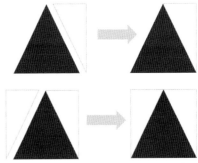

9. With the same process from steps 3 and 4, use one 6½" (16.5cm) red/pink improv triangle plus two 6½" (16.5cm) white triangle side units to make one red/pink improv triangle-in-a-square unit.

10. Place two 1½" (3.8cm) white squares on the top corners of a 2½" x 3½" (6.4 x 8.9cm) red/pink improv rectangle, right sides together, and sew from corner to corner. Trim the excess fabric, leaving ¼" (0.5cm) seam allowance, and press open to yield one heart top unit. Make two heart units.

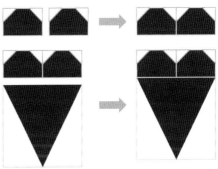

11. Lay out the heart top units side by side and sew them together as shown. Then sew the heart top units to the top of the triangle-in-a-square unit, with the point facing downward, to complete the heart block. The heart block should measure 6½" x 8½" (16.5 x 21.6cm), including seam allowances. Repeat steps 9–11 to make three total heart blocks.

Assemble the Quilt Top

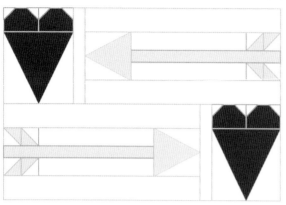

Quilt assembly diagram

12. Refer to the quilt assembly diagram to arrange the arrow blocks and heart blocks into three rows as shown. Sew the rows together to complete the quilt top.

Backing fabric and binding on the finished quilt.

Finish the Quilt

Refer to Finishing Your Quilt on page 112 for instructions on basting, quilting, and binding your quilt.

13. Cut the backing fabric into one piece, measuring 27" x 27" (68.6 x 68.6cm).

14. Layer the backing, batting, and quilt top and baste the layers together. Hand- or machine-quilt as desired. The heart and arrow blocks in Heartstruck are quilted with dense lines that echo the shapes of the blocks, and the white background is filled with stippling in soft pink thread to add a little extra interest.

15. Use the 2½" (6.4cm)–wide pink/red strips to make the binding, then attach it to the quilt.

Quilted lines and stippling add interest and texture.

Star Spangled

Whether you're decorating for the Fourth of July or planning a special gift for a veteran, this quilt packs the perfect dose of patriotism. It's created with basic quilting shapes, but the unique layout makes this flag stand out.

Color notes: Make this quilt with rich reds, medium and dark blues, and bright white for a crisp, classic look, or substitute a creamy beige or tan for a more historical feel.

MATERIALS

With the exception of improv pieces, yardage is based on 42" (106.7cm)–wide fabric.

- One improv piece, 11" x 28" (27.9 x 71.1cm), pieced from assorted red scraps for blocks
- One improv piece, 7" x 15" (17.8 x 38.1cm), pieced from assorted medium and dark blue scraps for blocks
- ⅓ yard (30.5cm) white fabric for blocks
- ¼ yard (22.9cm) dark blue fabric for binding
- ¾ yard (68.6cm) fabric for backing, or backing measuring 25" x 25" (63.5 x 63.5cm)
- 25" x 25" (63.5 x 63.5cm) piece of batting

CUTTING

All measurements include ¼" (0.5cm) seam allowances.

From the red improv piece, cut:
- Ten squares, 5½" (14cm)

From blue improv piece, cut:
- One square, 5½" (14cm)
- Four rectangles, 2" x 3½" (5.1 x 8.9cm)
- Two squares, 3½" (8.9cm)
- Four squares, 2" (5.1cm)

From the white fabric, cut:
- Eleven squares, 5½" (14cm)
- One square, 3½" (8.9cm)
- Eight squares, 2" (5.1cm)

From the dark blue fabric, cut:
- Three strips, 2½" x 42" (6.4 x 106.7cm) for binding

Note that improv pieces are represented by solid colors. Refer to page 9 for corner-to-corner sewing methods.

Make the Half-Square Triangles (HSTs)

1. Place a 5½" (14cm) improv square on one 5½" (14cm) white square, right sides together. Sew a ¼" (0.5cm) seam around all four edges.

2. Cut the sewn squares twice diagonally from corner to corner and press open to yield four HSTs. Trim each HST to 3½" (8.9cm) if necessary.

3. Follow steps 1 and 2 to pair the remaining 5½" (14cm) white squares with the 5½" (14cm) red and blue improv squares to make forty total red and four total blue HSTs (yields one extra red HST).

Make the Star Block

4. Place a 2" (3.8cm) white square on the corner of one 2" x 3½" (5.1 x 8.9cm) blue improv rectangle, right sides together, and sew from corner to corner. Trim the excess fabric, leaving ¼" (0.5cm) seam allowance, and press open.

5. Repeat this process on the adjoining corner. Trim the excess fabric, leaving ¼" (0.5cm) seam allowance, and press open to yield one Flying Geese unit. Make four total Flying Geese units.

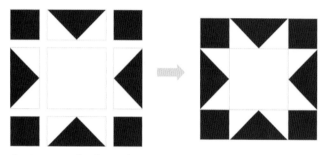

6. Lay out the four Flying Geese units, the 3½" (8.9cm) solid white square, and four 2" (5.1cm) blue improv squares into three rows as shown. Sew the rows together to complete the star block.

The stripes' wavy quilted lines echo the movement of a flag flying in the breeze.

Assemble the Quilt Top

Quilt assembly diagram

7. Refer to the quilt assembly diagram to arrange the HSTs, the 3½" (8.9cm) blue improv squares, and the star block into seven rows as shown. Sew the first two rows of 3½" (8.9cm) units together first, then join the star block after the rows are sewn. Sew the remaining rows of the quilt to complete the quilt top.

Finish the Quilt

Finishing Your Quilt on page 112 for instructions on basting, quilting, and binding your quilt.

8. Cut the backing fabric into one piece, measuring 25" x 25" (63.5 x 63.5cm).

9. Layer the backing, batting, and quilt top and baste the layers together. Hand- or machine-quilt as desired. The star in Star Spangled is finished with crosshatch quilting and stippling in the blue background, and the soft, wavy quilting in the red and white stripes adds the effect of motion, as if the flag were waving in the breeze.

10. Use the 2½" (6.4cm)–wide dark blue strips to make the binding, then attach it to the quilt.

FINISHED QUILT SIZE: 21" X 21" (53.3 X 53.3CM)

Birds of a Feather

I just love birds. They're delicate and colorful, and they're a lot of fun to watch. One of my favorite parts of spring is setting out my feeders and waiting for my backyard visitors. These bird silhouettes are a great way to welcome spring inside your home.

Color notes: Robin's egg blue and brown create a calm and soothing palette, and it's no surprise that so many people use these colors in their home decor. Birds of a Feather uses soft shades of blue and aqua, which create a perfect backdrop for the brown birds. This quilt would be equally beautiful with green scraps in the background to represent a forest, or you could keep it fresh and neutral with cream and tan scraps.

MATERIALS

With the exception of improv pieces, yardage is based on 42" (106.7cm)–wide fabric.

- Four improv pieces, 13" x 15" (33 x 38.1cm), each pieced from assorted light blue and aqua scraps for blocks
- ½ yard (45.7cm) brown fabric for blocks and binding (Robert Kaufman Fabrics' Kona® Cotton in Chestnut is shown)
- ¾ yard (68.6cm) fabric for backing, or backing measuring 27" x 27" (68.6 x 68.6cm)
- 27" x 27" (68.6 x 68.6cm) piece of batting

Quilting lines echo the shape of the bird and give the hint of a wing.

CUTTING

All measurements include ¼" (0.5cm) seam allowances.

From one light blue/aqua improv piece, cut:
- One rectangle, 9½" x 12½" (24.1 x 31.8cm)
- One rectangle, 4½" x 12½" (11.4 x 31.8cm)

From one light blue/aqua improv piece, cut:
- One rectangle, 7½" x 12½" (19.1 x 31.8cm)
- One rectangle, 6½" x 12½" (16.5 x 31.8cm)

From one light blue/aqua improv piece, cut:
- Two rectangles, 3½" x 9½" (8.9 x 24.1cm)
- Two rectangles, 4½" x 5½" (11.4 x 14cm)
- Four squares, 2½" (6.4cm)

From one light blue/aqua improv piece, cut:
- Two rectangles, 4½" x 6½" (11.4 x 16.5cm)
- Four squares, 4½" (11.4cm)
- Two rectangles, 1½" x 4½" (3.8 x 11.4cm)
- Two rectangles, 1½" x 3½" (3.8 x 8.9cm)
- Two squares, 1½" (3.8cm)

From the brown fabric, cut:
- One strip, 4½" x 42" (11.4 x 106.7cm); subcut:
  - Four rectangles, 4½" x 6½" (11.4 x 16.5cm)
  - Two rectangles, 2½" x 3½" (6.4 x 8.9cm)
  - Four squares, 2½" (6.4cm)
  - Two squares, 1½" (3.8cm)
  - Three strips, 2½" x 42" (6.4 x 106.7cm) for binding

FINISHED QUILT SIZE: 24" X 24" (61 X 61CM)

Make the Bird Blocks

Improv block components are represented by solid colors. Refer to page 9 for corner-to-corner sewing methods. This quilt requires sewing a mirror image of each component to create birds that face each other. Each step will include directions for sewing one unit and its mirror image in the same step.

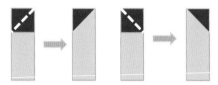

1. Place a 1½" (3.8cm) brown square on the corner of a 1½" x 3½" (3.8 x 8.9cm) improv rectangle, right sides together, and sew from corner to corner. Trim the excess fabric, leaving ¼" (0.5cm) seam allowance, and press open to make the beak. Repeat this process, sewing the corner square in the opposite direction, to make the mirror-image beak unit.

2. Place a 1½" (3.8cm) improv square on the top left corner of a 2½" x 3½" (6.4 x 8.9cm) brown rectangle, right sides together, and sew from corner to corner. Trim the excess fabric, leaving ¼" (0.5cm) seam allowance, and press open to make the head. Repeat this process, sewing the square to the top right corner to make the mirror-image head unit.

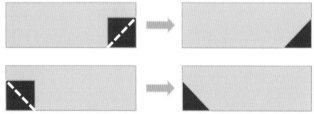

3. Place a 2½" (6.4cm) brown square on the bottom right corner of a 3½" x 9½" (8.9 x 24.1cm) improv rectangle, right sides together, and sew from corner to corner. Trim the excess fabric, leaving ¼" (0.5cm) seam allowance, and press open. Repeat this process, sewing the square to the bottom left corner to make the mirror-image unit.

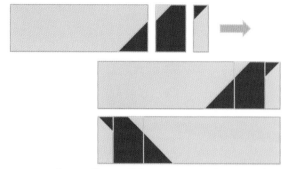

4. Lay out the 3½" x 9½" (8.9 x 24.1cm) rectangle from step 3, head unit, and beak unit as shown, then join the pieces together to create the head of the first bird. Repeat this process using the mirror-image units to create the head of the second bird.

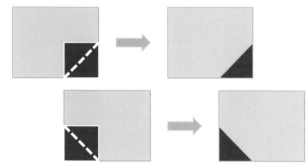

5. Place a 2½" (6.4cm) brown square on the bottom right corner of a 4½" x 5½" (11.4 x 14cm) improv rectangle, right sides together, and sew from corner to corner to make the wing tip. Trim the excess fabric, leaving ¼" (0.5cm) seam allowance, and press open. Repeat this process, sewing the corner square to the bottom left corner to make the mirror-image wing tip.

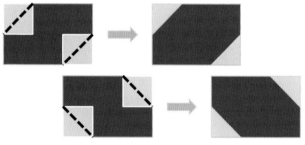

6. Place two 2½" (6.4cm) improv squares on opposite corners of one 4½" x 6½" (11.4 x 16.5cm) brown rectangle, right sides together, and sew from corner to corner. Trim the excess fabric, leaving ¼" seam allowance, and press open to make the body unit. Repeat this process, sewing the squares to the opposite corners to make the mirror-image body unit.

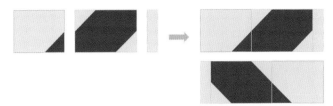

7. Lay out a wing tip unit, body unit, and one 1½" x 4½" (3.8 x 11.4cm) improv rectangle as shown. Join the pieces together to create the body of the bird. Repeat this process using the mirror-image units to create the mirror-image body of the second bird.

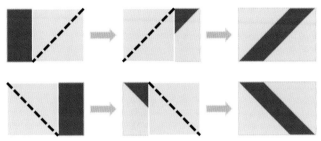

8. Place two 4½" (11.4cm) improv squares on opposite corners of a 4½" x 6½" (11.4 x 16.5cm) brown rectangle, right sides together, and sew from corner to corner. Trim the excess fabric, leaving ¼" (0.5cm) seam allowance, and press open to make the tail. Repeat this process, sewing the squares to the opposite corners to make the mirror-image tail unit.

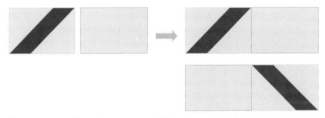

9. Sew a tail unit to one 4½" x 6½" (11.4 x 16.5cm) improv rectangle to create the tail of the first bird. Repeat this process to create the mirror-image tail of the second bird.

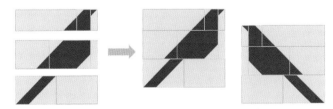

10. Lay out the head, body, and tail of the first bird in three rows as shown and join the pieces together to create the first bird block. Repeat this process using the mirror-image units to complete the mirror-image bird block. The two bird blocks should each measure 11½" x 12½" (29.2 x 31.8cm).

Assemble the Quilt Top

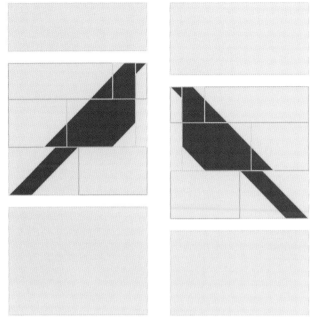

Quilt assembly diagram

11. Refer to the quilt assembly diagram to sew the 4½" x 12½" (11.4 x 31.8cm) improv rectangle to the top of the first bird, and the 9½" x 12½" (24.1 x 31.8cm) improv rectangle to the bottom of the bird. Then sew the 6½" x 12½" (16.5 x 31.8cm) improv rectangle to the top of the second bird, and the 7½" x 12½" (19.1 x 31.8cm) improv rectangle to the bottom of the second bird. Sew the two birds together to complete the quilt top.

Finish the Quilt

Refer to Finishing Your Quilt on page 112 for instructions on basting, quilting, and binding your quilt.

12. Cut the backing fabric into one piece, measuring 27" x 27" (68.6 x 68.6cm).

13. Layer the backing, batting, and quilt top and baste the layers together. Hand- or machine-quilt as desired. Birds of a Feather is quilted with lines within each bird, echoing the shape of the bird, and filled with paisley quilting on the improv background.

14. Use the 2½" (6.4cm)–wide brown strips to make the binding, then attach it to the quilt.

Fall Foliage

When the heat of summer gives way to crisp fall air, the trees put on a spectacular show of color. The bold maple leaf in this quilt captures all the feelings and charm of autumn, and it makes me want to take a drive to see the colorful foliage.

Color notes: Batik fabrics are dyed with a special process that gives them a very distinctive look, almost like a watercolor painting. This quilt uses all batik scraps, which adds amazing depth of color to the maple leaf. Don't worry if you don't have batik scraps. Any scraps in warm shades of brown, orange, red, and yellow will create an effect just as beautiful.

MATERIALS

With the exception of improv pieces, yardage is based on 42" (106.7cm)–wide fabric.

- One improv piece, 11" x 16" (27.9 x 40.6cm), pieced from assorted brown, orange, red, and yellow scraps for blocks
- ⅓ yard (30.5cm) solid tan fabric for blocks and border (Robert Kaufman Fabrics' Kona® Cotton in Khaki is shown)
- ⅛ yard (11.4cm) brown or one rectangle 1" x 12" (2.5 x 30.5cm) brown for the leaf stem
- ¼ yard (22.9cm) fabric for binding, or refer to the instructions on page 117 to create a scrappy pieced binding measuring 78" (198.1cm)
- ⅓ yard (30.5cm) fabric for backing, or backing measuring 21" x 21" (53.3 x 53.3cm)
- 21" x 21" (53.3 x 53.3cm) piece of batting

CUTTING

All measurements include ¼" (0.5cm) seam allowances.

From the improv piece, cut:
- Two squares, 5½" (14cm)
- Eight squares, 3½" (8.9cm)

From the tan background fabric, cut:
- One strip, 2" x 42" (5.1 x 106.7cm); subcut:
  - Two rectangles, 2" x 15½" (5.1 x 39.4cm), for side borders
- One strip, 2" x 42" (5.1 x 106.7cm); subcut:
  - Two rectangles, 2" x 18½" (5.1 x 47cm), for top and bottom borders
- One strip 7½" x 42" (19.1 x 106.7 cm); subcut:
  - One square, 7½" (19.1cm)
  - Two squares, 5½" (14cm)
  - Five squares, 3½" (8.9cm)

For a solid binding, from the binding fabric, cut:
- Two strips, 2½" x 42" (6.4 x 106.7cm), for binding

FINISHED QUILT SIZE: 18" X 18" (45.7 X 45.7CM)

Note that improv pieces are represented by solid colors. Refer to page 9 for corner-to-corner sewing methods.

Make the Half-Square Triangles (HSTs)

1. Place a 5½" (14cm) improv square on a 5½" (14cm) tan square, right sides together. Sew a ¼" (0.5cm) seam around all four edges.

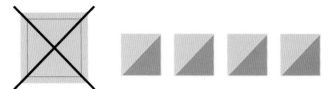

2. Cut the sewn squares twice diagonally from corner to corner and press open to yield four HSTs. Trim each HST to 3½" (8.9cm) if necessary. Repeat this process to make eight total HSTs, each measuring 3½" (8.9cm).

Fold the solid brown rectangle and the cut piece of the solid tan square in half to find the center point of each piece. Use a pin to hold the solid brown rectangle in place so it stays centered while you are sewing. Use a square ruler with a bias line to keep the solid brown rectangle centered when trimming to size.

Make the Stem

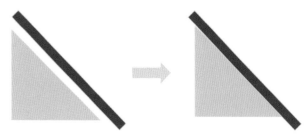

3. Cut the 7½" (19.1cm) solid tan square in half diagonally. Sew the 1" x 12" (2.5 x 30.5cm) solid brown rectangle to one of the halves and press open.

4. Sew the second half of the 7½" (19.1cm) tan square to the other side of the solid brown rectangle as shown and press open. Trim the stem unit to 6½" (16.5cm), keeping the solid brown rectangle centered in the block.

Assemble the Maple Leaf Block

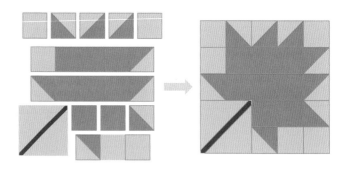

5. Refer to the quilt assembly diagram to lay out the HSTs, improv 3½" (8.9cm) squares, solid tan 3½" (8.9cm) squares, and stem block into five rows as shown. Join the first three rows together. For rows four and five, sew the 3½" (8.9cm) units together first and then join the stem block. Then sew all five rows of the quilt together.

Assemble the Quilt Top

Quilt assembly diagram

6. Sew one 2" x 15½" (5.1 x 39.4cm) tan rectangle to each side of the quilt, then sew one 2" x 18½" (5.1 x 47cm) tan rectangle to the top and bottom of the quilt.

Finish the Quilt

Refer to Finishing Your Quilt on page 112 for instructions on basting, quilting, and binding your quilt.

7. Cut the backing fabric into two equal pieces, measuring 12" x 21" (30.5 x 53.3cm) each. Sew the two pieces together to make the backing.

8. Layer the backing, batting, and quilt top and baste the layers together. Hand- or machine-quilt as desired. Fall Foliage is quilted with an all-over wood grain design, adding to the outdoorsy feel of the design. The quilting adds tons of texture and really brings the maple leaf to life.

9. Use the 2½" (6.4cm)–wide solid or scrap strips to make the binding, then attach it to the quilt.

Backing fabric and binding on the finished quilt.

Wood-grain quilting adds outdoor charm to the autumn leaf.

Ornamental

Christmas is one time of year when I go a little crazy with the decorations. I put up four Christmas trees, each with a different theme, and cram much Christmas cheer into my home as I possibly can. There are so many different styles of Christmas décor: fancy, whimsical, traditional, woodsy … the list goes on, and I am an equal opportunity lover of all of it. The ornaments in this quilt use a mix of several different styles of Christmas scraps, and they all play very nicely together.

Color notes: Christmas fabrics often have a mix of red and green in them, but usually there is a predominant color. When sorting your scraps, if you come across a fabric that features both colors equally, just go with your gut and don't worry too much about it. Your ornaments will look great with a bit of variation. The background of this quilt is a subtle metallic gold. If there's ever a time when you can get away with a little extra glam, it's Christmas, and the metallic fabric is such a fun way to show off the ornaments. If you don't want to use a metallic fabric, a cream or white background will be just as pretty.

MATERIALS

With the exception of improv pieces, yardage is based on 42" (106.7cm)–wide fabric.

- One improv piece, 7" x 13" (17.8 x 33cm), pieced from assorted green Christmas scraps for blocks
- One improv piece, 6" x 7" (15.2 x 17.8cm) pieced from assorted red Christmas scraps, for blocks
- ⅔ yard (70cm) metallic gold fabric for blocks and background (Glimmer Solids by Cloud9 Fabric in Champagne is shown)
- ⅛ yard (11.4cm) solid gray fabric for blocks (Robert Kaufman Fabrics' Kona® Cotton in Graphite is shown)
- ⅛ yard (11.4cm) or two rectangles of solid red fabric, 1½" x 6½" (3.8 x 16.5cm), for blocks (Robert Kaufman Fabrics' Kona® Cotton in Rich Red is shown)
- ⅛ yard (11.4cm) or one rectangle of solid green fabric, 1½" x 5½" (3.8 x 14cm), for blocks (Robert Kaufman Fabrics' Kona® Cotton in Basil is shown)
- ¼ yard (22.9cm) red fabric for binding
- ¾ yard (68.6cm) fabric for backing, or backing measuring 27" x 27" (68.6 x 68.6cm)
- 27" x 27" (68.6 x 68.6cm) piece of batting
- Triangle-in-a-square ruler set, such as Tri-Recs

CUTTING

All measurements include ¼" (0.5cm) seam allowances. See Triangle-in-a-Square Blocks on page 10 for instructions on cutting the triangles and triangle side units. When cutting the triangle side units, if you are using a print fabric in the background, keep the fabric folded in half, right sides together, and cut two mirror-image side triangles at the same time.

From the red improv piece, cut:
- One rectangle, 3½" x 5½" (8.9 x 14cm)
- Two triangles, 3½" (8.9cm)

From the green improv piece, cut:
- Two squares, 6½" (16.5cm)

From the solid red fabric, cut:
- Two rectangles, 1½" x 6½" (3.8 x 16.5cm)

From the solid green fabric, cut:
- One rectangle, 1½" x 5½" (3.8 x 14cm)

From the solid gray fabric, cut:
- One strip, 1" x 42" (2.5 x 106.7cm); subcut:
  - One rectangle, 1" x 14½" (2.5 x 36.8cm)
  - One rectangle, 1" x 11½" (2.5 x 29.2cm)
  - One rectangle, 1" x 5½" (2.5 x 14cm)
  - Two rectangles, 1½" x 2" (3.8 x 5.1cm)

(Cutting list continued on page 88)

FINISHED QUILT SIZE: 23" X 23" (58.4CM)

(Cutting list continued from page 86)

From the metallic gold background fabric, cut:
- One strip, 5½" x 42" (14 x 106.7cm); subcut:
  - One rectangle, 5½" x 8½" (14 x 21.6cm)
  - Two rectangles, 3¾" x 5½" (9.5 x 14cm)
  - Two rectangles, 4¼" x 11½" (10.8 x 29.2cm)
- One strip, 4¼" x 42" (10.8 x 106.7cm); subcut:
  - Two rectangles, 4¼" x 14½" (10.8 x 36.8cm)
  - One rectangle, 2½" x 8½" (6.4 x 21.6cm)
- One strip, 7½" x 42" (19.1 x 106.7cm); subcut:
  - One rectangle, 7½" x 9½" (19.1 x 24.1cm)
  - Four rectangles, 1½" x 3¾" (3.8 x 9.5cm)
  - Four rectangles, 1½" x 6½" (3.8 x 16.5cm)
  - Two squares, 3½" (8.9cm)
  - Four rectangles, 2½" x 3½" (6.4 x 8.9cm)
- One strip, 3½" x 42" (8.9 x 106.7cm); subcut:
  - Four triangle side units, 3½" (8.9cm)
  - Four squares, 2½" (6.4cm)
  - Two squares, 2" (5.1cm)
  - Two rectangles, 1½" x 3½" (3.8 x 8.9cm)
  - Four squares, 1½" (3.8cm)

From the binding fabric, cut:
- Three strips, 2½" x 42" (6.4 x 106.7cm), for binding

Note that improv pieces are represented by solid colors. Refer to page 9 for corner-to-corner sewing methods.

Make the Ornament Blocks

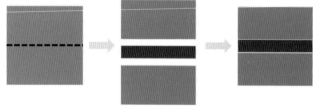

1. Cut one 6½" (16.5cm) green improv square in half to yield two pieces, each measuring 3¼" x 6½" (8.3 x 16.5cm), and sew one 1½" x 6½" (3.8 x 16.5cm) red rectangle between the two halves. Trim the unit to 6½" (16.5cm) square. Make two identical units.

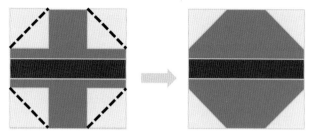

2. Place a 2½" (6.4cm) gold square on the corner of a 6½" (16.5cm) green improv square, right sides together, and sew from corner to corner. Trim the excess fabric, leaving ¼" (0.5cm) seam allowance, and press open. Repeat this process on the remaining three corners to make the first green ornament.

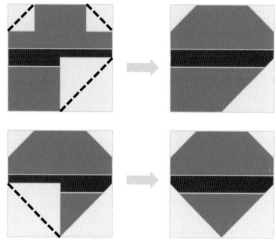

3. Place two 2" (5.1cm) gold squares on the top corners of the remaining 6½" (16.5cm) green improv square, right sides together, and sew from corner to corner. Then use the same process to sew one 3½" (8.9cm) gold square to the bottom right corner of the square. Trim the excess fabric from all three corners, leaving ¼" (0.5cm) seam allowance, and press open.

4. Sew a 3½" (8.9cm) gold square to the final corner of the green improv square. Trim the excess fabric, leaving ¼" (0.5cm) seam allowance, and press open to make the second green ornament.

5. Sew a 1½" x 3¾" (3.8 x 9.5cm) rectangle to each side of a gray 1½" x 2" (3.8 x 5.1cm) rectangle to make the ornament cap. Make two ornament caps total.

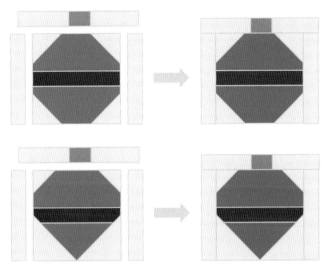

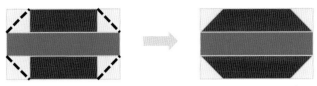

8. Place a 1½" (3.8cm) gold square on the corner of the red rectangle, right sides together, and sew from corner to corner. Trim the excess fabric, leaving ¼" (0.5cm) seam allowance, and press open. Repeat this process on the remaining three corners.

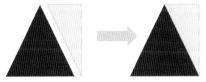

6. Lay out the first green improv ornament, two 1½" x 6½" (3.8 x 16.5cm) gold rectangles, and an ornament cap as shown and join the pieces together to finish the first green ornament block. Repeat this process to make the second green ornament block.

9. Sew a gold side triangle to a 3½" (8.9cm) red improv triangle and press open.

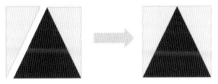

7. Cut the 3½" x 5½" (8.9 x 14cm) red improv rectangle in half to yield two pieces, each measuring 1¾" x 5½" (4.4 x 14cm), and sew the 1½" x 5½" (3.8 x 14cm) green rectangle between the two halves. Trim the unit to 3½" x 5½" (8.9 x 14cm).

10. Sew a second gold side triangle to the opposite side of the red improv triangle and press open to make one complete triangle-in-a-square unit, measuring 3½" (8.9cm). Make two total triangle-in-a-square units.

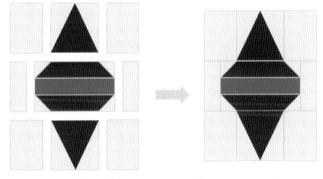

The rich red ornament really stands out against the metallic gold background.

11. Lay out the red improv rectangle, two triangle-in-a-square units, two 1½" x 3½" (3.8 x 8.9cm) gold rectangles, and four 2½" x 3½" (6.4 x 8.9cm) gold rectangles into three rows as shown. Sew the pieces into rows, then sew the rows together to make the red ornament block.

Make the Ornament Strings

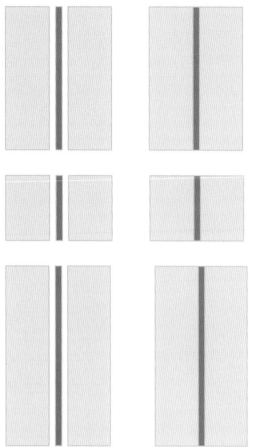

12. Sew a 4¼" x 11½" (10.8 x 29.2cm) gold rectangle to each side of the 1" x 11½" (2.5 x 29.2cm) gray rectangle to complete the string for the first green ornament. Then sew one 3¾" x 5½" (9.5 x 14cm) gold rectangle to each side of the 1" x 5½" (2.5 x 14cm) gray rectangle to complete the string for the middle ornament. Use the same process to sew one 4¼" x 14½" (10.8 x 36.8cm) gold rectangle to each side of the 1" x 14½" (2.5 x 36.8cm) gray rectangle to complete the string for the last green ornament.

Sew the Quilt Sections

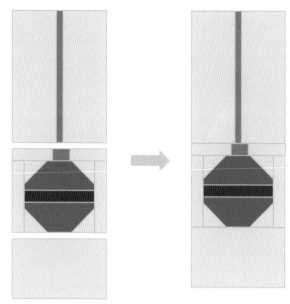

13. Lay out the 11½" (29.2cm) string unit, the first green ornament, and the 5½" x 8½" (14 x 21.6cm) gold rectangle as shown and sew the pieces together to complete the first ornament section.

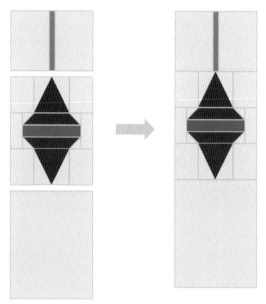

14. Lay out the 5½" (14cm) string unit, the red ornament, and the 7½" x 9½" (19.1 x 24.1cm) gold rectangle as shown and sew the pieces together to complete the middle ornament section.

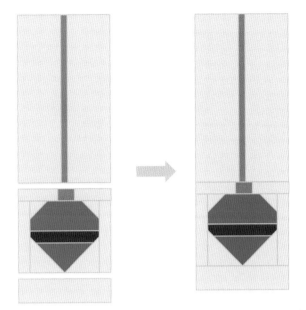

15. Lay out the 14½" (36.8cm) string unit, the second green ornament, and the 2½" x 8½" (6.4 x 21.6cm) gold rectangle as shown and sew the pieces together to complete the last ornament section.

Assemble the Quilt Top

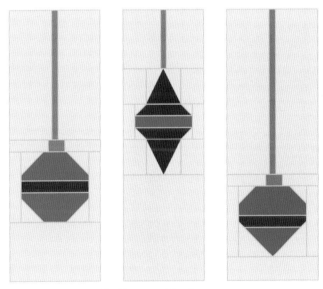

Quilt assembly diagram

16. Refer to the quilt assembly diagram to arrange the three ornament sections in order as shown, then sew the sections together to complete the quilt top.

Finish the Quilt

Refer to Finishing Your Quilt on page 112 for instructions on basting, quilting, and binding your quilt.

17. Cut the backing fabric into one piece, measuring 27" x 27" (68.6 x 68.6cm).

18. Layer the backing, batting, and quilt top and baste the layers together. Hand- or machine-quilt as desired. Ornamental is quilted with lines in the ornaments to add definition, and the background is filled with stippling.

19. Use the 2½" (6.4cm)–wide red strips to make the binding, then attach it to the quilt.

Stippling in the background helps define the ornaments.

CHAPTER 5

Standards with a Twist

With hundreds of quilt blocks in the public domain, everyone is bound to have a favorite. These traditional blocks never go out of style, and they're another way for your scraps to really shine. The designs in this section use improv piecing to put an updated spin on the classics, and even though the blocks have been around for decades, these scrappy quilts are creative and unique.

Churn, Churn, Churn

Churn Dash blocks have been around almost as long as quilting itself, and they are one of my favorite quilt blocks. These three Churn Dash blocks are nested together and put a fresh twist on this classic block, making it really special.

> **Color notes:** Three shades of pink steal the show in this quilt. When scraps are divided into light, medium, and dark, the result is almost a 3D effect that gives definition to each Churn Dash—or choose three coordinating colors for a completely different look.

MATERIALS

With the exception of improv pieces, yardage is based on 42" (106.7cm)–wide fabric.

- One improv piece, 7" x 7" (17.8cm x 17.8cm), pieced from assorted light pink scraps for blocks
- One improv piece, 7" x 14" (17.8 x 35.6cm), pieced from assorted medium pink scraps for blocks
- One improv piece, 13" x 24" (33 x 61cm), pieced from assorted dark pink scraps for blocks
- ½ yard (45.7cm) gray fabric for blocks (Robert Kaufman Fabrics' Kona® Cotton in Medium Grey is shown)
- ¼ yard (22.9cm) pink fabric for binding
- ¾ yard (68.6cm) fabric for backing, or backing measuring 27" x 27" (68.6 x 68.6cm)
- 27" x 27" (68.6 x 68.6cm) piece of batting

CUTTING

All measurements include ¼" (0.5cm) seam allowances.

From the light pink improv piece, cut:
- One square, 3½" (8.9cm)
- Four rectangles, 1¼" x 3½" (3.2cm x 8.9cm)

From the medium pink improv piece, cut:
- One square, 5½" (14cm)
- Four rectangles, 2" x 6½" (5.1 x 16.5cm)

From the dark pink improv piece, cut:
- One square, 9¾" (24.8cm)
- Four rectangles, 3½" x 12½" (8.9 x 31.8cm)

From the gray background fabric, cut:
- One strip, 9¾" x 42" (24.8 x 106.7cm); subcut:
  - One square, 9¾" (24.8cm)
  - Four rectangles, 3½" x 12½" (8.9 x 31.8cm)
- One strip 5½" x 42" (14 x 106.7cm); subcut:
  - One square, 5½" (14cm)
  - Four rectangles, 2" x 6½" (5.1 x 16.5cm)
  - Two squares, 3½" (8.9cm)
  - Four rectangles, 1¼" x 3½" (3.2cm x 8.9cm)

From the pink binding fabric, cut:
- Three strips, 2½" x 42" (6.4 x 106.7cm) for binding

FINISHED QUILT SIZE: 24" X 24" (61 X 61CM)

Note that improv pieces are represented by solid colors. Refer to page 9 for corner-to-corner sewing methods.

Make the Half-Square Triangles (HSTs)

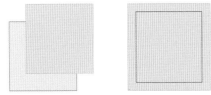

1. Place a 3½" (8.9cm) improv square on one 3½" (8.9cm) gray square, right sides together. Sew a ¼" (0.5cm) seam around all four edges of the squares.

2. Cut the sewn squares twice diagonally from corner to corner and press open to yield four light pink HSTs. Trim each HST to 2" (5.1cm) if necessary.

3. Repeat the process in steps 1 and 2 with the 5½" (14cm) squares to make four 3½" (8.9cm) medium pink HSTs. Then, in the same manner, use the 9¾" (24.8cm) squares to make four 6½" (16.5cm) dark pink HSTs.

Defined points give the Churn Dash block its well-known look.

Make the Side Units

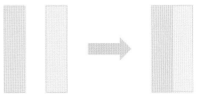

4. Sew a 1¼" (3.2cm) gray rectangle to a 1¼" (3.2cm) light pink rectangle and press. Make four total light pink side units.

5. Repeat this process using the 2" x 6½" (5.1 x 16.5cm) rectangles to make four medium pink side units. Then, in the same manner, use the 3½" x 12½" (8.9 x 31.8cm) rectangles to make four dark pink side units.

Assemble the Quilt Top

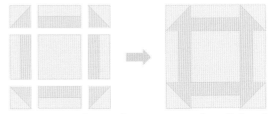

6. Lay out a 3½" (8.9cm) gray square, four light pink side units, and four light pink HSTs into three rows as shown. Join the pieces together to make the light pink Churn Dash block.

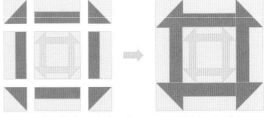

7. Lay out the light pink Churn Dash block, four medium pink side units, and four medium pink HSTs into three rows as shown. Join the pieces together to complete the medium pink Churn Dash block.

Piecing the quilt block with the points on top will help ensure that your HST points are nice and crisp.

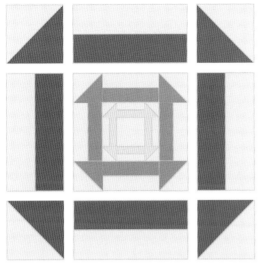

8. Lay out the medium pink Churn Dash block, four dark pink side units, and four dark pink HSTs into three rows as shown. Join the pieces together to complete the quilt top.

Finish the Quilt

Refer to Finishing Your Quilt on page 112 for instructions on basting, quilting, and binding your quilt.

9. Cut the backing fabric into one piece, measuring 27" x 27" (68.6 x 68.6cm).

10. Layer the backing, batting, and quilt top and baste the layers together. Hand- or machine-quilt as desired. Churn, Churn, Churn is quilted with an all-over box stipple pattern, created with intersecting straight lines and sharp angles, to echo the sharp points and straight lines in the quilt.

11. Use the 2½" (6.4cm)–wide pink strips to make the binding, then attach it to the quilt.

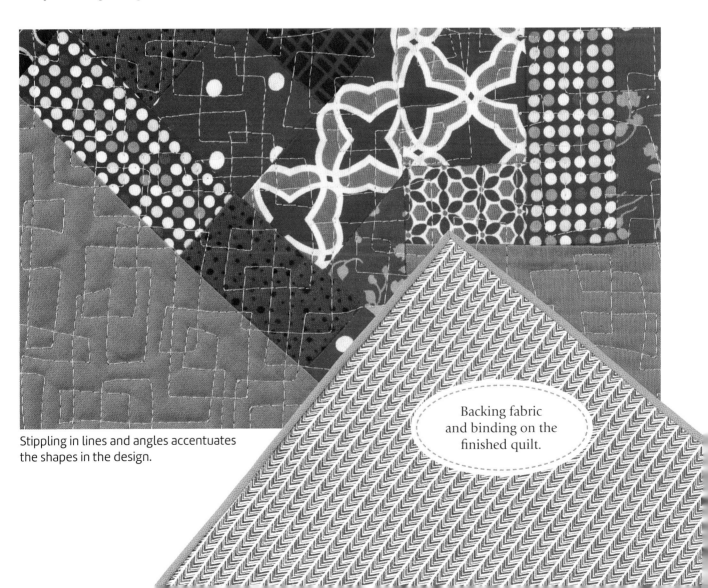

Stippling in lines and angles accentuates the shapes in the design.

Backing fabric and binding on the finished quilt.

Sunset Crossing

The sunset over the ocean is one of the most gorgeous sights I've ever experienced. I would watch the warm, peachy glow of the sun wash over the cool water of the Gulf of Mexico every day if I could. These traditional Crossroads blocks play with those colors to create a quilt as soothing as an evening on the beach.

> **Color notes:** The layout of the dark and light colors gives a lot of movement to the quilt, and the bright white background makes Sunset Crossing feel very summery. Choosing shades of aqua/teal can be tricky, but don't overthink it. It's OK if some fabrics are more blue in tone and others are more green in tone. As long as the color is somewhere between blue and green, use it! This variation will add texture to your improv piecing.

MATERIALS

With the exception of improv pieces, yardage is based on 42" (106.7cm)–wide fabric.

- One improv piece, 7" x 18" (17.8 x 45.7cm), pieced from assorted dark blue scraps for blocks
- One improv piece, 7" x 18" (17.8 x 45.7cm), pieced from assorted aqua and teal scraps for blocks
- ¼ yard (22.9cm) dark coral fabric for blocks and binding (Robert Kaufman Fabrics' Kona® Cotton in Melon is shown)
- ⅛ yard (11.4cm) light coral/peach fabric for blocks (Robert Kaufman Fabrics' Kona® Cotton in Peach is shown)
- ⅓ yard (30.5cm) white fabric for blocks and background
- ⅓ yard (30.5cm) fabric for backing, or backing measuring 21" x 21" (53.3 x 53.3cm)
- 21" x 21" (53.3 x 53.3cm) piece of batting

CUTTING

All measurements include ¼" (0.5cm) seam allowances.

From the dark blue improv piece, cut:
- Ten squares, 3½" (8.9cm)

From the aqua/teal improv piece, cut:
- Ten squares, 3½" (8.9cm)

From the dark coral fabric, cut:
- Two strips, 2½" x 42" (6.4 x 106.7cm) for binding
- Two squares, 3½" (8.9cm)
- Ten squares, 2" (5.1cm)

From the light coral/peach fabric, cut:
- Two squares, 3½" (8.9cm)
- Ten squares, 2" (5.1cm)

From the white background fabric, cut:
- One strip, 3½ x 42" (8.9 x 106.7cm); subcut:
  - Four rectangles, 3½" x 6½" (8.9 x 16.5cm)
  - Four squares, 3½" (8.9cm)
- Three strips, 2" x 42" (5.1 x 106.7cm); subcut:
  - Sixty squares, 2" (5.1cm)
- One strip, 2" x 42" (5.1 x 106.7cm); subcut:
  - Eight rectangles, 2" x 3½" (5.1 x 8.9cm)

FINISHED QUILT SIZE: 18" X 18" (45.7 X 45.7CM)

Make the Crossroads Blocks

Improv block components are represented by solid colors.
Refer to page 9 for corner-to-corner sewing methods.

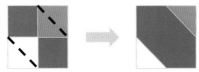

1. Place a 2" (5.1cm) dark coral square and a 2" (5.1cm) white square on opposite corners of a 3½" (8.9cm) blue improv square, right sides together, and sew from corner to corner. Trim the excess fabric, leaving ¼" (0.5cm) seam allowance, and press open.

2. Repeat this process, sewing 2" (5.1cm) white squares to the remaining corners of the blue improv square. Trim the excess fabric, leaving ¼" (0.5cm) seam allowance, and press open. Make ten total dark blue units.

3. In the same manner as steps 1 and 2, sew a 2" (5.1cm) light coral/peach square and three 2" (5.1cm) white squares to a 3½" (8.9cm) aqua/teal improv square. Make ten total aqua/teal units.

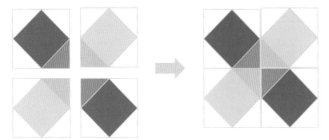

4. Lay out two dark blue units and two aqua/teal units with the solid coral and peach corners pointing toward the center of the block as shown. Join the pieces together to make the block. Make five total Crossroads blocks.

Make the Half-Square Triangles (HSTs)

5. Place a 3½" (8.9cm) dark coral square on a 3½" (8.9cm) white square, right sides together. Sew a ¼" (0.5cm) seam around all four edges of the squares.

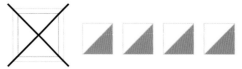

6. Cut the sewn squares twice diagonally from corner to corner and press open to yield four HSTs. Trim each HST to 2" (5.1cm) if necessary. Repeat to make eight total dark coral HSTs. Repeat the steps with light coral/peach and white 3½" (8.9cm) squares to make eight total light coral/peach 2" (5.1cm) HSTs.

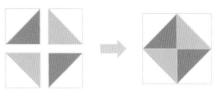

7. Lay out two 2" (5.1cm) dark coral HSTs and two 2" (5.1cm) light coral/peach HSTs as shown, then sew the four HSTs together to yield one unit. Make four total HST units.

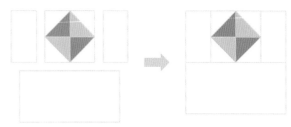

8. Lay out one HST unit, two 2" x 3½" (5.1 x 8.9cm) white rectangles, and one 3½" x 6½" (8.9 x 16.5cm) white rectangle as shown. Join the pieces together to create one HST block.

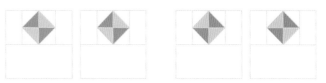

9. Repeat this process to make four total HST blocks: two HST blocks with dark coral in the top left corner and two HST blocks with light coral/peach in the top left corner. This placement is necessary to keep the color arrangement consistent in the quilt.

Assemble the Quilt Top

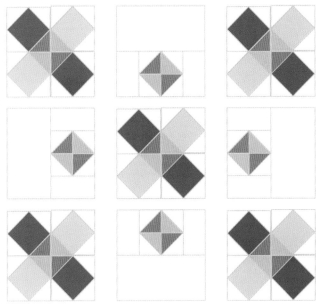

Quilt assembly diagram

10. Refer to the quilt assembly diagram to arrange the five Crossroads blocks and four HST blocks into three rows as shown. Take note of the placement of the dark and light coral HST blocks to keep the color arrangement consistent throughout the quilt. Sew the rows together to complete the quilt top.

Finish the Quilt

Refer to Finishing Your Quilt on page 112 for instructions on basting, quilting, and binding your quilt.

11. Cut the backing fabric into two equal pieces, measuring 12" x 21" (30.5 x 53.3cm) each. Sew the two pieces together to make the backing.

12. Layer the backing, batting, and quilt top and baste the layers together. Hand- or machine-quilt as desired. The dark blue and aqua/teal improv blocks in Sunset Crossing are quilted with diagonal lines in opposing directions to create an X pattern in the blocks. The X theme is continued within the coral sections, which are quilted in a crosshatch pattern, as though the blue and aqua lines cross in the center of the block. The white background of the quilt is filled with a stipple, and the curved lines add contrast to the straight quilting lines in the blocks.

13. Use the 2½" (6.4cm)–wide dark coral strips to make the binding, then attach it to the quilt.

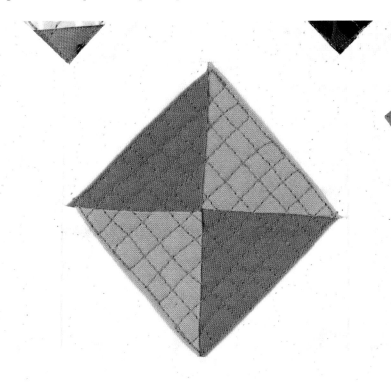

Backing fabric and binding on the finished quilt.

The coral blocks are quilted with crosshatching, while curved, stippled lines in the background add contrast.

Positivity

We can all use a little extra positivity from time to time, and this simple, fun quilt does the trick. With just simple squares, it goes together in a flash, but the creative layout and negative space give this classic quilt an unexpected twist.

> **Color notes:** This quilt is easy to customize with your two favorite colors to match a specific decor or even to celebrate your favorite sports team.

MATERIALS

With the exception of improv pieces, yardage is based on 42" (106.7cm)–wide fabric.

- One improv piece, 10" x 13" (25.4 x 33cm), pieced from assorted purple scraps for blocks
- One improv piece, 10" x 15" (25.4 x 38.1cm), pieced from assorted gray scraps for blocks
- ⅓ yard (30.5cm) white fabric for blocks
- ¼ yard (22.9cm) purple fabric for binding
- ⅔ yard (61cm) fabric for backing, or backing measuring 24" x 24" (61 x 61cm)
- 24" x 24" (61 x 61cm) piece of batting

CUTTING

All measurements include ¼" (0.5cm) seam allowances.

From the purple improv piece, cut:
- Nineteen squares, 2½" (6.4cm), yields one extra

From gray improv piece, cut:
- Twenty-three squares, 2½" (6.4cm), yields one extra

From the white background fabric, cut:
- Four strips, 2½" x 42" (6.4 x 106.7cm); subcut:
  - Fifty-eight squares, 2½" (6.4cm), yields six extra

From the purple fabric, cut:
- Three strips, 2½" x 42" (6.4 x 106.7cm), for binding

Piecing the entire top with squares helps to keep everything lined up when sewing the quilt top.

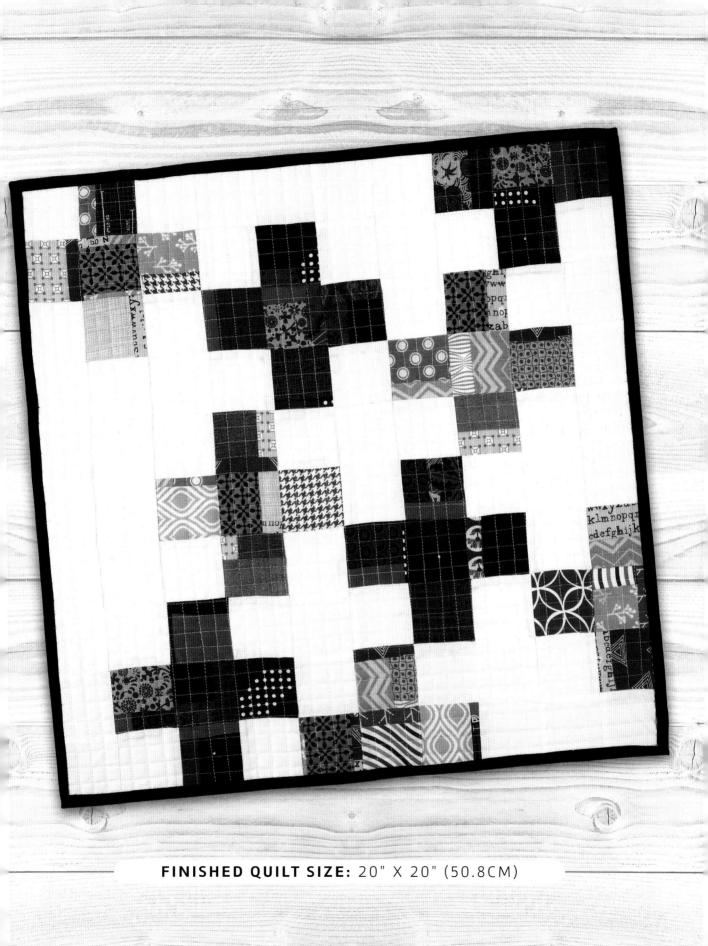

FINISHED QUILT SIZE: 20" X 20" (50.8CM)

Assemble the Quilt Top

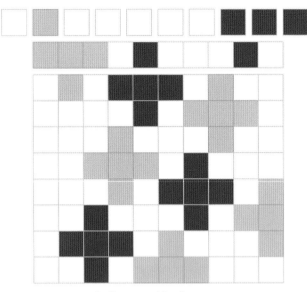

Quilt assembly diagram

1. Refer to the quilt assembly diagram to arrange the white squares, purple improv squares, and gray improv squares into rows. Sew the squares into rows, then sew the rows together to complete the quilt top.

Finish the Quilt

Refer to Finishing Your Quilt on page 112 for instructions on basting, quilting, and binding your quilt.

2. Cut the backing fabric into one piece, measuring 24" x 24" (61 x 61cm).

3. Layer the backing, batting, and quilt top and baste the layers together. Hand- or machine-quilt as desired. Positivity was quilted with simple grid lines using a walking foot. The seams were used as a guide to create half-inch grid squares.

4. Use the purple 2½" (6.4cm)–wide strips to make the binding, then attach it to the quilt.

If you are worried about keeping your squares aligned, you can sew the quilt top in quarters as four 10-inch (25.4cm) blocks instead of rows. Then join the four blocks together to make the quilt top.

The colored squares and linear quilting emphasize the grid–like pattern of the design.

All Dressed Up

The Bowtie block is a traditional quilt block with tons of possibilities. Bowtie blocks are cute on their own, but when put together, they make a fun, rounded shape. Just a little bit of negative space added to these blocks makes All Dressed Up much more interesting than a Bowtie quilt with a traditional layout.

Color notes: This one is all about the blues! Sort your scraps into dark, medium, and light to achieve the color gradient effect, which gives this quilt dimension. The smoky gray background fabric shows off all these blues beautifully.

MATERIALS

With the exception of improv pieces, yardage is based on 42" (106.7cm)–wide fabric.

- One improv piece, 10" x 15" (25.4 x 38.1cm), pieced from assorted light blue scraps for blocks
- One improv piece, 10" x 15" (25.4 x 38.1cm), pieced from assorted medium blue scraps for blocks
- One improv piece, 10" x 21" (25.4 x 53.3cm), pieced from assorted dark blue scraps for blocks
- ½ yard (45.7cm) gray fabric for blocks and background (Robert Kaufman Fabrics' Kona® Cotton in Silver is shown)
- ¼ yard (22.9cm) blue fabric for binding (Robert Kaufman Fabrics' Kona® Cotton in Stratosphere is shown)
- ¾ yard (68.6cm) of fabric for backing, or backing measuring 27" x 27" (68.6 x 68.6cm)
- 27" x 27" (68.6 x 68.6cm) piece of batting

CUTTING

All measurements include ¼" (0.5cm) seam allowances.

From *each* light blue and medium blue improv piece, cut:

- Sixteen squares, 2½" (6.4cm)
- Sixteen squares, 1½" (3.8cm)

From the dark blue improv piece, cut:

- Twenty-four squares, 2½" (6.4cm)
- Twenty-four squares, 1½" (3.8cm)

From the gray background fabric, cut:

- Four strips, 2½" x 42" (6.4 x 106.7cm); subcut:
  - Fifty-six squares, 2½" (6.4cm), yields eight extra
- One strip, 4½" x 42" (11.4 x 106.7cm); subcut:
  - Eight squares, 4½" (11.4cm)

From the blue binding fabric, cut:

- Three strips, 2½" x 42" (6.4 x 106.7cm), for binding

Backing fabric and binding on the finished quilt.

Make the Blocks

Improv block components are represented by solid colors. Refer to page 9 for corner-to-corner sewing methods.

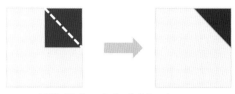

1. Place one 1½" (3.8cm) dark blue improv square on the corner of a 2½" gray (6.4cm) square and sew from corner to corner. Trim the excess fabric, leaving ¼" (0.5cm) seam allowance, and press open. Make two total Bowtie block units.

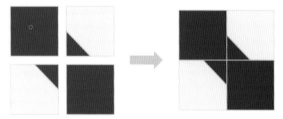

2. Lay out the two Bowtie block units and two 2½" (6.4cm) dark blue improv squares as shown, then join the pieces to make the block. Repeat this process to make twelve dark blue blocks, eight medium blue blocks, and eight light blue blocks.

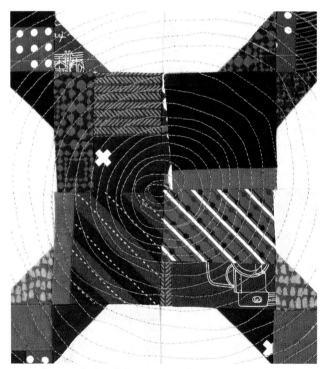

Free-form spiral quilting that leads into a vortex in the center of the design lends texture and movement.

Assemble the Quilt Top

Quilt assembly diagram

3. Refer to the quilt assembly diagram to arrange the dark blue, medium blue, and light blue Bowtie blocks and the gray 4½" (11.4cm) squares into six rows, each containing six blocks, as shown. Sew the rows together to complete the quilt top.

Finish the Quilt

Refer to Finishing Your Quilt on page 112 for instructions on basting, quilting, and binding your quilt.

4. Cut the backing fabric into one piece, measuring 27" x 27" (68.6 x 68.6cm).

5. Layer the backing, batting, and quilt top and baste the layers together. Hand- or machine-quilt as desired. All Dressed Up is quilted with a giant, dense free-form spiral, which echoes the rounded shapes in the design. It has overlapping lines in the center, giving the quilt extra texture and the feeling of a vortex in the middle of the quilt.

6. Use the 2½" (6.4cm)–wide blue strips to make the binding, then attach it to the quilt.

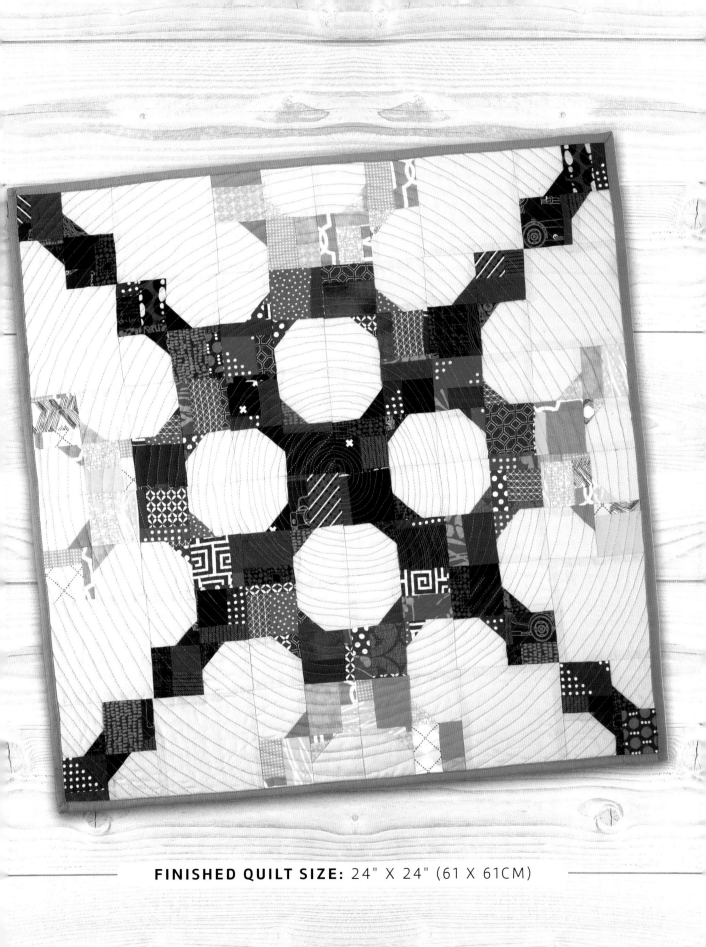

FINISHED QUILT SIZE: 24" X 24" (61 X 61CM)

Shockwave

With its layered look, the Pineapple block is a timeless design that delivers major impact. This single large block is a spin on the traditional version, and because this one is made with Flying Geese, it is much easier to put together.

> **Color notes:** This quilt is a great place to play with the color spectrum. Shockwave uses the warm side of the color wheel, but it would be equally spectacular with cool colors. The navy blue background is a perfect contrast to the fiery palette.

MATERIALS

With the exception of improv pieces, yardage is based on 42" (106.7cm)–wide fabric.

- One improv piece, 12" x 12" (30.5 x 30.5cm), pieced from assorted yellow scraps for blocks
- One improv piece, 9" x 17" (22.9 x 43.2cm), pieced from assorted orange scraps for blocks
- One improv piece, 7" x 13" (17.8 x 33cm), pieced from assorted red scraps for blocks
- One improv piece, 8" x 10" (20.3 x 25.4cm), pieced from assorted pink and berry purple scraps for blocks
- ⅝ yard (57.2cm) dark blue fabric for blocks and background (Robert Kaufman Fabrics' Kona® Cotton in Nightfall is shown)
- ¼ yard (22.9cm) yellow fabric for binding
- ¾ yard (68.6cm) fabric for backing, or backing measuring 26" x 26" (66 x 66cm)
- 26" x 26" (66 x 66cm) piece of batting

CUTTING

All measurements include ¼" (0.5cm) seam allowances.

From the yellow improv piece, cut:
- One square, 11½" (29.2cm)

From the orange improv piece, cut:
- Four rectangles, 4½" x 8½" (11.4 x 21.6cm)

From the red improv piece, cut:
- Four rectangles, 3½" x 6½" (8.9 x 16.5cm)

From the pink/purple improv piece, cut:
- Four rectangles, 2½" x 4½" (6.4 x 11.4cm)
- Four rectangles, 1½" x 2½" (3.8 x 6.4cm)

From the blue fabric, cut:
- One strip, 11½" x 42" (29.2 x 106.7cm); subcut:
  - One square, 11½" (29.2cm)
  - Eight squares, 4½" (11.4cm)
  - Twelve squares, 1½" (3.8cm)
- One strip, 7" x 42" (17.8 x 106.7cm); subcut:
  - Thirteen squares, 2½" (6.4cm)
  - Eight squares, 3½" (8.9cm)
  - Eight rectangles, 1½" x 3½" (3.8 x 8.9cm)

From the yellow fabric, cut:
- Three strips, 2½" x 42" (6.4 x 106.7cm), for binding

FINISHED QUILT SIZE: 22" X 22" (55.9 X 55.9CM)

Improv pieces are represented by solid colors.
Refer to page 9 for corner-to-corner sewing methods.

Make the Flying Geese

1. Place one 4½" (11.4cm) blue square on the corner of one 4½" x 8½" (11.4 x 21.6cm) orange improv rectangle, right sides together. Sew from corner to corner. Trim away the excess fabric, leaving ¼" (0.5cm) seam allowance, and press open.

2. Repeat this process on the adjoining corner as shown to yield one Flying Geese unit. Make four total orange Flying Geese units, each measuring 4½" x 8½" (11.4 x 21.6cm), including seam allowances.

3. Repeat the process in steps 1 and 2 to sew two 3½" (8.9cm) blue squares to each 3½" x 6½" (8.9 x 16.5cm) red improv rectangle to make four total red Flying Geese units.

4. Use the same process to sew two 2½" (6.4cm) blue squares to each 2½" x 4½" (6.4 x 11.4cm) pink improv rectangle to make four larger pink Flying Geese. Then sew the 1½" (3.8cm) blue squares to the 1½" x 2½" (3.8 x 6.4cm) pink improv rectangles to make four smaller pink Flying Geese units.

To save a lot of time, sew the corner squares to one side of all the Flying Geese at once, then press all of them before sewing the corners to the second side.

Make the Half-Square Triangles (HSTs)

5. Lay one 11½" (29.2cm) yellow improv square on one 11½" (29.2cm) blue square, right sides together. Sew a ¼" (0.5cm) seam around the edges of the squares.

6. Cut the sewn squares twice diagonally from corner to corner and press open to yield four HSTs. Trim each HST to 7½" (19.1cm) if necessary.

Make the Center Unit

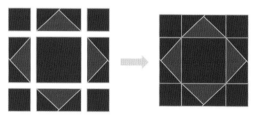

7. Lay out one 2½" (6.4cm) blue square, four smaller pink Flying Geese, and four 1½" (3.8cm) blue squares into three rows as shown, then sew the rows together.

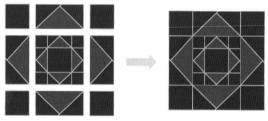

8. Lay out the unit from step 7, four larger pink Flying Geese, and four 2½" (6.4cm) blue squares into three rows as shown, then sew the rows together to complete the center unit.

Make the Side Units

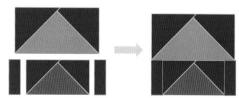

9. Sew a 1½" x 3½" (3.8 x 8.9cm) blue rectangle to each side of one red Flying Geese unit. Then sew one orange improv Flying Geese unit to the top to complete one side unit. Make four total side units.

Assemble the Quilt Top

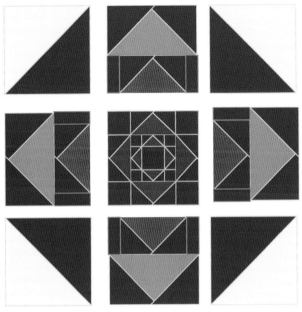

Quilt assembly diagram

10. Refer to the quilt assembly diagram to arrange the yellow improv HSTs, four side units, and center unit into three rows as shown, then sew the rows together to complete the quilt top.

Finish the Quilt

Refer to Finishing Your Quilt on page 112 for instructions on basting, quilting, and binding your quilt.

11. Cut the backing fabric into one piece, measuring 26" x 26" (66 x 66cm).

12. Layer the backing, batting, and quilt top and baste the layers together. Hand- or machine-quilt as desired. Shockwave is quilted with dense lines that follow the shape of the piecing.

13. Use the 2½" (6.4cm)–wide strips to make the binding, then attach it to the quilt.

Backing fabric and binding on the finished quilt.

The quilted lines follow the shape of the design.

CHAPTER 6

Finishing Your Quilt

Once your quilt top is complete, you're ready to turn that beauty into a finished mini quilt that's ready to gift or display. The basics for finishing a quilt are the same no matter the pattern or size, and these guidelines will have you admiring your improv masterpiece in no time.

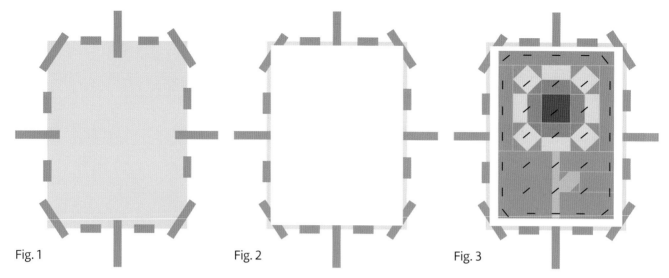

Fig. 1 Fig. 2 Fig. 3

Basting is the process of putting the three layers of your quilt together.

Make the Backing

The backing of your quilt can be as simple or as intricate as you like. The instructions given with each project are for sewing a simple backing made with a single fabric, but once you get comfortable, you can piece your backing with several fabrics or even make a double-sided quilt! One of the best things about sewing mini quilts is that they are small, so I usually have all the materials I need on hand. Sometimes that means a pieced backing is the way to go, and I like to think of it as an extra little surprise when you flip the quilt over. Whatever you decide, just be sure to make the backing about 3–4 inches (7–11cm) larger than the quilt top, giving you a bit of extra width around the entire quilt.

Choose Your Batting

The batting you choose will make a big difference in the overall feel of your finished quilt, so choose wisely! My favorite batting is either Warm & Natural® or Warm & White®, both by The Warm® Company. These are 100% cotton, low-loft battings that have great weight without too much puffiness. I use these battings in my larger projects as well, and I love to use leftover pieces from larger projects for my mini quilts. I do know some quilters who prefer batting that is a little puffier, like $^8/_{20}$ batting. These are all high-quality choices, so it really comes down to personal preference.

Baste the Layers

There's no doubt about it—for quilts of any size, great quilting starts with great basting. Basting is the process of putting the three layers of your quilt (top, batting, and backing) together so that you can stitch through all three layers. Without proper basting, the layers can shift around during quilting, which causes wrinkles and puckers, so take your time with this step to keep your quilt nice and smooth. There are several different basting methods, including using basting spray, safety pins, or even a needle and thread, and different quilters swear by different methods. I find safety-pin basting to be the most effective, and it isn't too tedious. Here's how to do it:

1. Start by laying out your pressed quilt backing on a table or the floor, wrong side up. Pull the backing taut (but don't stretch it!) and use painter's tape or masking tape to keep it in place. Work all the way around the backing, pulling taut and taping, until the backing is smooth. Mark the center point of each side of the backing with a longer piece of tape to help you keep everything aligned later. (Fig. 1)

2. Lay your batting on top of the backing and gently smooth out any wrinkles. Use the tape markers to help you center the batting, and trim away any excess that extends over the edge of the backing. (Fig. 2)

3. Add your pressed quilt top, right side up, to finish the quilt sandwich. Again, use your tape markers to center the top with the backing, making sure that it is straight, and gently smooth it out so that it is "stuck" to the batting.

4. Use safety pins to hold all three layers together. Start pinning in the center of the quilt and work outward, smoothing any additional wrinkles as you go. Pin every 4–5 inches (10–13cm), covering the entire mini quilt sandwich. (Fig. 3)

5. Trim away any excess batting and backing, making sure to leave about 1½–2 inches (4–5cm) of "wiggle room" all the way around the quilt top.

Time to Quilt!

It's thrilling to finish a quilt top, but the design really comes to life with the quilting, and this is where mini quilts need a little extra consideration.

- **Proportion is important**—Because mini quilts are small by definition, the quilting will stand out much more than it does on a larger quilt. You'll notice that the projects in this book are quilted rather densely to keep the scale of the entire quilt consistent. Keep in mind that quilting stitches "pull" on your quilt, so very dense quilting can shrink your quilt a tiny bit—don't be confused if your finished quilt measures ¼"–½" (0.5–1.5cm) smaller after quilting. It's totally worth it!

- **Enhance the quilt; don't compete with it**—Most often when making a mini quilt, I match my quilting thread to the individual colors in the quilt top. This helps the thread blend right into each section. It still adds plenty of texture but doesn't create too much busyness in the overall quilt. When I opt to use a single color for all-over quilting, I choose the color that blends best with everything, usually a soft gray.

The great thing about a mini quilt is that, even with dense quilting, the task at hand is manageable because it's on a small piece. I finished each of the quilts in this book on my domestic machine, and not a single one of them is perfect. Nothing handmade ever is, and that's part of the charm!

If you're looking at your basted mini quilt and feeling a bit overwhelmed, don't worry. When I taught elementary school, and a student would get frustrated, I used to ask, "How do you eat an elephant?" Of course, the answer is, "One bite at a time." The kids always found that expression funny, but the lesson is equally true in this scenario. Mentally divide your quilt into sections, take it one "bite" at a time, and you'll find that the task will feel more manageable.

This book is not intended to be a comprehensive guide to machine quilting, but I'll cover a few important basics. If you need a complete primer on finishing your quilt on a domestic machine, there are many books and online videos that exclusively address the topic.

WALKING FOOT QUILTING

Many beautiful quilts are quilted with simple lines using a walking foot, and if you're a beginner, this is a great place to start. You can quilt with all-over, evenly spaced lines, lines following the quilt design, a grid or crosshatch pattern, or even random lines throughout the quilt. If needed, use masking tape or painter's tape on your quilt as a guide for your lines. Even the gentle

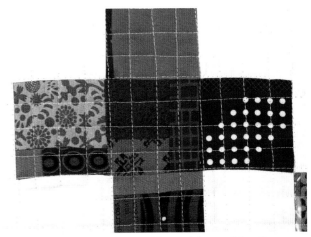

Crisp grid lines are easy to achieve with a walking foot.

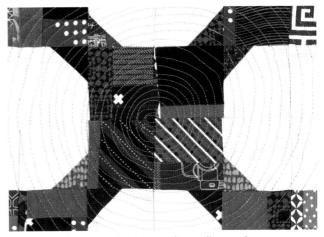

A walking foot can also be used to quilt gentle curves, as in a continuous spiral.

curve in a giant continuous spiral can be done with your walking foot and a little patience.

The importance of your walking foot cannot be stressed enough here. All sewing machines have feed dogs (those little teeth on your stitch plate) that pull the fabric through. The problem with using a regular presser foot to quilt is that the feed dogs can only grab the bottom layer of your quilt sandwich, causing the top to shift while quilting. The walking foot feeds the top and bottom layers evenly and solves this problem, so it is absolutely essential for this kind of quilting.

FREE-MOTION QUILTING

For free-motion quilting, you'll need a free-motion quilting foot (or darning foot), which will allow you to move your quilt in any direction to create all kinds of fun designs. The quilts in this book show a variety of free-motion motifs, including stippling, pebbles, swirls, boxes, wavy lines, wood grain, and paisleys, often with several mixed in a single quilt. If free-motion quilting is

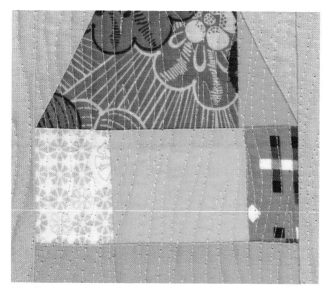

Use free–motion quilting to create texture, as shown by these relaxed, wavy lines.

unfamiliar territory for you, mini quilts are the perfect place to practice!

Regardless of the motif you choose, practice first by sketching your design on paper so you can get a good idea of how to use the design to fill a space with one continuous line. It may sound silly, but it helps! Then, if you'd like to try out the design, use some scrap batting and fabric to make a practice quilt sandwich. Finally, when you feel comfortable, stitch the design onto your quilt, working with a small section at a time. Some quilters like to start in the center of the quilt at the top, working in rows up and down the quilt, and others prefer to divide their quilt into quarters and work that way. Whichever you choose, just relax, take it in pieces, and quilt a little at a time.

Trim and Square

When you've finished quilting, use a rotary cutter and ruler to trim away the excess batting and backing, straightening the edge of the quilt if necessary. A square ruler is helpful for making sure the corners of your quilt are square.

Binding Your Quilt

Binding is the process of finishing the edges of your quilt. The method I discuss here is called *double-fold binding*. It is easy and durable, and it finishes the edges nicely. The patterns in this book are written using 2½" (6.4cm) binding strips, but I must confess that for a mini quilt, I often cut my strips to 2" (5.1cm) or 2¼" (5.7cm) to give a more narrow finish to the edge. Start

with the traditional 2½" (6.4cm) width and, as you feel more comfortable, move to a slightly thinner strip. If not, a 2½" (6.4cm) strip works perfectly well.

1. Per the pattern instructions, cut the specified number of 2½" x 42" (6.4 x 106.7cm) strips and join them end to end, right sides together, to create a single long strip.

2. Press the strip in half lengthwise, wrong sides together, pressing the joining seams open as you go. The binding should measure 1¼" (3.2cm) wide, and the unfinished seams should be inside the fold.

Leave a 6" loose binding tail before sewing

3. Sew the binding to the edge of the quilt on the back side, ¼" (0.5cm) from the edge of the quilt, with the raw edge of the binding strip facing the edge of the quilt. Begin sewing your binding in the middle of one side of the quilt; leave about a 6" (15cm) tail of loose binding before your stitching begins.

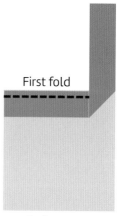

First fold

4. When you approach the corner, stop sewing ¼" (0.5cm) before the corner, backstitch, and remove the quilt from under the needle. Fold your binding up, creating a 45-degree angle from the corner of the quilt.

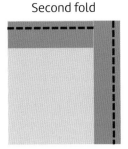

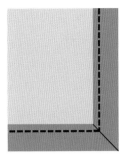

5. Keep your finger on the first fold to hold it in place, then fold the binding a second time to align it with the next side of your quilt. Sew ¼" (0.5cm) from the edge through the fold, backstitch, and continue sewing the binding down the next edge of the quilt.

6. Repeat this process to continue around the quilt. When you approach your starting point, stop sewing about 6 inches (15cm) before reaching the loose binding tail and backstitch.

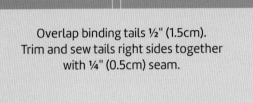

Overlap binding tails ½" (1.5cm).
Trim and sew tails right sides together
with ¼" (0.5cm) seam.

7. Align the two loose binding ends and overlap them. Your end binding tail should overlap the beginning binding tail by ½" (1.5cm). Trim away the excess binding and sew the two ends together, right sides together, with a ¼" (0.5cm) seam. (Note: Pinning is very helpful for this step.) Press the seam open and press the binding fold again if necessary. Finish sewing the binding to the edge of the quilt and backstitch to secure it.

8. Pull the folded binding edge to the front of the quilt, just past the first seam, and stitch it to the front of the quilt, sewing as closely to the edge of the fold as possible. Fold and miter the corners as you sew around them. Backstitch at the beginning and end to secure your stitches.

I bind all of my quilts 100 percent by machine using this method, but if you prefer to not have any visible binding stitches, sew the binding to the front of the quilt first, then stitch to the back of the quilt by hand, hiding your stitches inside the fold of the binding.

Scrappy Binding

Because this book is all about using scraps, feel free to create a scrappy binding with different fabric strips of various lengths, measuring 2½" (6.4cm) wide. Measure the length of all sides of your quilt and add them together to determine the length of your binding. Sew your scrappy binding strips together until the binding is long enough to go around the entire quilt, plus 6" (15.2cm) extra just to be safe. A scrappy binding can disappear into the quilt if there is improv piecing in the background, or it can add a little extra interest.

In the Face the Sun quilt, the binding seems to disappear.

Ideas for Displaying Mini Quilts

MAKE A HANGING SLEEVE

To display your quilt on a wall by hanging it from a dowel or rod, you will need a hanging sleeve. This not only looks nice but also avoids having to make pinholes in the corners of your quilt. Hanging sleeves are quick and easy to make.

1. Cut a 6–8" (15–20cm) strip of fabric, about 1½ (3.8cm) inches longer than the top of your quilt.
2. Fold each short side over twice, about ½ inch (1.5cm), and sew the fold down to finish the short edges. After this step, the strip should be a little shorter than the top of your quilt.
3. Fold the strip in half lengthwise, with the finished edge facing outward. Sew down the length of the strip to create a long tube.
4. Turn the tube right side out and press it. Hand-stitch along the top and bottom of the tube to secure it to the back of your quilt, just under the binding at the top of the quilt.

I like to sew hanging sleeves with large stitches that can be easily snipped and pulled out. That way, if I decide to display a quilt in a different way, I can remove the sleeve in minutes. For a more permanent sleeve, sew the top of the tube underneath the binding of your mini quilt, and use hand stitching only for attaching the bottom of the sleeve.

MAKE A PILLOW

Mini quilts make great throw pillows for beds, chairs, or sofas. Once your mini is quilted, turning it into a pillow is a snap! These instructions are for a pillow cover with an envelope closure on the back and a binding edge.

1. Measure the length and width of your pillow. Divide the length in half and add 5" (12.7cm) for the overlapping backing. For instance, if your mini quilt is 18" (45.7cm) long, you will need 9" (22.9cm) plus 5" extra, for a total of 14" (35.6cm).
2. Cut two pieces of fabric measuring the exact width of your mini quilt x the calculated measurement from the previous step. So, for an 18" (45.7cm)–wide mini quilt, you would cut two pieces, each 18" x 14" (45.7 x 35.6cm).
3. Fold one edge of each backing piece twice along the width, then sew the fold to finish one raw edge of each backing piece. Don't worry about the other edges!
4. Lay your mini quilt face down on a table, then lay the backing pieces, right sides out, on top of the quilt. The raw edges of the backing fabric should be aligned with the raw edges of the quilt, and the finished edges should be overlapped across the back. Pin the backing fabric in place and sew the backing fabric all the way around the quilt with a ¼" (0.5cm) seam.
5. Follow the standard binding instructions on page 116 to enclose the raw edges, then insert a pillow form. If you can't find a pillow form with the exact measurements of your pillow, using one that is a bit larger will work. It will give you a very puffy pillow, which is great!

Raw edges

Finished backing edges overlap

A pillow with an envelope closure is an easy way to display a mini quilt.

¼" (0.5cm) seam sewn around all four edges

Size It Up!

Once you are comfortable with improv piecing in little quilts, you're ready to jump into making bigger improv projects to really put a dent in your scrap collection. There are a few easy ways to do this:

- **Treat the mini quilts like individual blocks.** Use multiple mini quilts to create larger projects. A set of three or four minis would make a generously sized table runner or topper, or you could use even more minis to make a bigger quilt.
- **Double the size.** Many of the designs in the mini quilts would look lovely as large, single blocks in baby or throw-sized quilts. To size up a quilt block for this purpose, take the *finished size* of a block in a mini quilt, double it, and then add ½" (1.5cm) seam allowance. So a 2" (5.1cm) finished piece in a mini quilt would be cut at 4½" (11.4cm) for a baby quilt, to finish at 4" (10.2cm). Use this method to double the length and width of an entire mini quilt, easily turning a 24" (61cm) mini into a 48" (122cm) quilt, an 18" (45.7cm) mini into a 36" (91.4cm) quilt, and so on. Triple the measurements to go even bigger.
- **Play with other traditional blocks.** Improv piecing is definitely not a one-trick pony. It is a method that you can apply to almost any quilt block, but two-color blocks work best. Pick your favorite block design and substitute improv piecing for one of the colors.
- **Use patterns.** If quilt math is not your strong suit, and you're ready to jump into improv on a larger scale, check out my first book, *Stash Statement* (Martingale, 2018). The book is similar in technique but contains twelve patterns for lap-sized quilts with step-by-step instructions. It is chock full of helpful hints for improv piecing on a larger scale.

No matter how you choose to expand your improv horizons, just have fun with it. You can feel great knowing that you're putting your treasured scraps to good use and making something awesome!

Laundering

Even quilts used just for display can get dirty, especially if they're used on a tabletop. For a quilt made with saturated colors and a lot of contrast, color-catcher sheets can absorb excess dyes and give you a little insurance against bleeding colors. Although high-quality fabrics rarely have this problem, it's better to be safe than sorry! Use a few color-catcher sheets in the first couple of washes and wash your quilts in cold water to help them stay pristine and your colors vibrant.

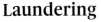

Wash your quilts in cold water to help keep your colors vibrant.

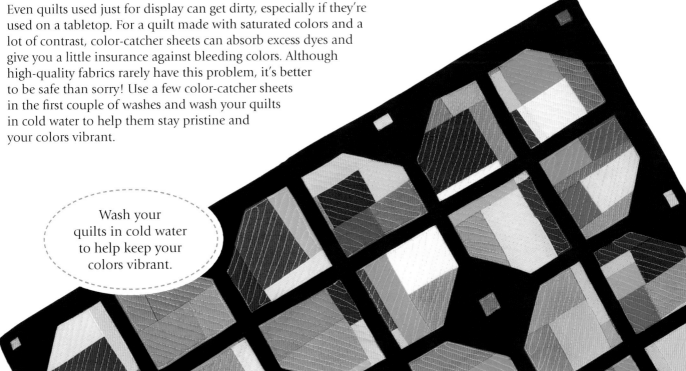

Acknowledgments

Without the love and support of my husband, Brandon, there is no way I could have made the transition from teaching elementary school to quilting and designing full time. It was this career change that has led to writing my books, and I have unending gratitude for his encouragement.

Much of the quilting and writing process for *Scrappy Improv Quilting* occurred during the COVID-19 pandemic quarantine, and I would have been lost without the help of my son, Nicholas, who always stepped up to help out with our Boxer puppy, Finn. Puppies are a lot of work, and I don't think I could have devoted the necessary time to this book without his puppy-wrangling help.

Thanks also to my mom, grandmother, and friend Janet for their honest opinions and listening ears when I needed to bounce ideas off of someone during the writing and design process.

And finally, I would be remiss if I didn't express my thanks to my editors at Landauer/Fox Chapel books, Amelia and Amy, along with all of the other helpful folks at Fox Chapel, in helping this book become a reality.

About the Author

Kelly Young is a quilter, author, pattern designer, and quilt teacher. A former elementary teacher who has been making quilts for over 20 years, Kelly traded her classroom full of children for a classroom full of quilters and began traveling to teach and design patterns full-time in 2015.

With a passion for making scrappy quilts, she tries to pack as many fabrics as possible into her designs. She loves blending carefree improv piecing with the comfortable structure of a quilt pattern, and this led her to further explore the improv technique, first in her debut book, *Stash Statement* (Martingale, 2018), and now in a fresh, new direction with *Scrappy Improv Quilting*. As a former teacher, Kelly enjoys encouraging quilters to try new skills, building their confidence, and helping them have fun in the process!

Kelly lives in Germantown, Tennessee where she is a member of the Memphis Area Modern Quilt Guild. To learn more about Kelly and her classes, patterns, tutorials, and more, visit her website, *www.MyQuiltInfatuation.com*, her Etsy shop (*www.etsy.com/shop/MyQuiltInfatuation*) or her Instagram (*@myquiltinfatuation*).